Living

Leo Butler

methuen | drama

LONDON • NEW YORK • OXFORD • NEW DELHI • SYDNEY

METHUEN DRAMA
Bloomsbury Publishing Plc, 50 Bedford Square, London, WC1B 3DP, UK
Bloomsbury Publishing Inc, 1359 Broadway, New York, NY 10018, USA
Bloomsbury Publishing Ireland, 29 Earlsfort Terrace, Dublin 2, D02 AY28, Ireland

BLOOMSBURY, METHUEN DRAMA and the Methuen Drama logo are trademarks of Bloomsbury Publishing Plc.

First published in Great Britain 2026

A catalogue record for this book is available from the British Library.

Library of Congress Control Number: 2026934361

ISBN: PB: 978-1-3506-3527-2
ePDF: 978-1-3506-3528-9
eBook: 978-1-3506-3529-6

Series: Modern Plays

Typeset by Mark Heslington Ltd, Scarborough, North Yorkshire

For product safety related questions contact productsafety@bloomsbury.com.

To find out more about our authors and books visit www.bloomsbury.com and sign up for our newsletters.

Dedicated to

JUDITH BUTLER

(1948–2025)

Living had its world premiere at Sheffield Theatre, Playhouse, on 14 March 2024 with the following cast and creative team:

Harki Bhambra as Rajesh and others

Michelle Bonnard as Jules and others

Samuel Creasey as Mike

Kenny Doughty as Brian

Andrew Macklin as Sean and others

Melina Sinadinou as Maya and others

Abby Vicky-Russell as Rebecca

Liz White as Kathy

Writer **LEO BUTLER**

Director **ABIGAIL GRAHAM**

Set and Costume Designer **SARAH BEATON**

Lighting Designer **MATT HASKINS**

Sound Designer **ANNIE MAY FLETCHER**

Video Designer **DAN LIGHT**

Movement and Intimacy Director **ANGELA GASPARETTO**

Casting Director **SOPHIE PARROTT CDG**

Fight Director **BRET YOUNT**

Associate Director **GITIKA BUTTOO**

Wigs, Hair and Make Up Designer **DARREN WARE**

Assistant Director **GEORGIE BOTHAM**

About Sheffield Theatres

Sheffield Theatres is home to four theatres: the Crucible, the Sheffield landmark with a world-famous reputation; the Tanya Moiseiwitsch Playhouse, an intimate, versatile space for getting closer to the action; the gleaming Lyceum, the beautiful proscenium that hosts the best of the UK's touring shows, and the Montgomery, a theatre and arts centre with a longstanding history of championing children's creativity.

Sheffield Theatres is the ticket to big names and local heroes, timeless treasures and new voices, and each year welcomes over 400,000 audience members.

With a long-standing reputation for bold new work, many multi-award-winning shows have been made in Sheffield including *Life of Pi* and *Everybody's Talking About Jamie* which have both enjoyed West End and international transfers before returning to the theatres as part of UK tours.

Other recent transfers include the acclaimed *Accidental Death of an Anarchist*, and the sensational Sheffield-set new musical *Standing at the Sky's Edge* which transferred to the National Theatre and the West End in 2024. Jack Holden and Ed Stambollouian's *KENREX* had a sell-out run in the Playhouse in autumn 2024, transferring to Southwark Playhouse Borough in February 2025 and more recently to The Other Palace for Christmas 2025–26.

Committed to investing in the creative leaders of the future, Sheffield Theatres' dedicated talent development hub, The Bank, supports a new cohort of emerging theatre-makers from the region every year.

In January 2025, the Montgomery Theatre and Arts Centre joined the Sheffield Theatres family of venues. A leading arts centre for children, families and community groups in Yorkshire, the Montgomery is also home to many of Sheffield Theatres participatory strands for children and young people.

Sheffield Theatres Crucible Trust is a Registered Charity. No. 1120640 and is a company limited by guarantee No. 6035820

Sheffield Theatres Trust is a Registered Charity No. 257318 and is a company limited by guarantee No. 932254

ACKNOWLEDGEMENTS

My agent, Giles Smart, for always believing in the play.

My thanks and gratitude to John Tiffany for his notes and support on the early drafts, and to Katherine Kelly and the actors who took part in the early R&D workshops.

Thanks also to everyone who generously offered feedback and enthusiasm over the past few years, and who – whether they meant to or not – helped bring the play to the stage: Tom Goodman Hill, Huss Garbiya, Dave Lovatt, David Eldridge, Morgan Lloyd Malcolm, and the members of the Marlowe Theatre's Advanced Playwriting Group 2025.

My brother, Matt Butler, and our dad, Bill Butler, for their inspiration and love.

Elizabeth Newman for saying YES, for her passion and no-nonsense approach, and for bringing the play home.

Nick Stevenson, and all the team at Sheffield Theatres, for looking after the play and the company.

All the actors – Liz, Kenny, Abby, Harki, Samuel, Michelle, Melina and Andrew – for their brilliance and creativity, and for making the characters wholly their own; the entire creative team for their conjury and invention; and our outstanding stage managers.

Our audacious director, Abigail Graham. I'd pretty much given up on playwriting, so thank you for raising the play from the dead and bringing it back to life with such vision, compassion and humour.

Finally, Nazzi and Bea, for everything and more – for shouldering me through all the ups and downs, and for reminding me what it's all for.

Living

Characters

Brian
Kathy
Mike
Rebecca
Rajesh
Sean
Jules
Nina
Hanif
Melissa
Maya
Safiya

and others.

Settings

A living room. Sheffield, South Yorkshire. 1969–2024.

Doubling

For a cast of eight the doubling of parts is as follows.

Kathy
Brian / Estate Agent
Mike
Rebecca
Taxi Driver / Hanif / College Friend / Labour Councillor / Rajesh
Old Woman / Jules /Aunty Gayle / Nicole /College Friend / Melissa / Safiya
Sean / Geoff / Phillip / College Friend /Davey-Boy/ Shan / Young Man
Karen / Kay / Janey C. / Nina / Maya / Young Woman

Note on Text

All scenes should flow effortlessly into each other (in as much of an inventive or simple way that you can find).

Dialogue and entrances/exits at the beginnings and endings of scenes are **written in bold** *to help you find the speed and rhythm of the scene changes.*

As usual a solidus / denotes an interruption, but there are other interruptions that you'll find that I haven't marked.

Some sections of dialogue run side by side. Have a go. Sometimes it really matters that certain lines ping out, sometimes it can be a fun jumble.

It would be ideal if you could use the pieces of music DREAM 13 (MINUS EVEN) by MAX RICHTER and THIS WOMAN'S WORK by KATE BUSH which feature, respectively, towards the end of Act 1 and Act 2.

Imitations of real people – such as Boris Johnson or various people on news reports – shouldn't be played as caricatures (for cheap laughs).

Act One

1969

Monday July 21st (3.00 am)

The curtains in the living room are open, the lights are off.

Moonlight shines in.

The Moon landing is being broadcast by the BBC on a vintage 1969 radio.

A **Woman** *in her seventies, in her night dress/dressing gown, sits in the armchair, smoking a cigarette, watching the moonlight as she listens to the broadcast.*

Long pause.

A sound like broken glass from the front of the house, offstage.

Woman Bill?

The **Woman** *slowly gets up from the sofa and crosses the room.*

She steps into the hallway, exits the living room.

Woman (*as she exits*) Bill, love, **are yer –**

1970

Monday March 16th (Morning)

Kathy (20) *is heavily pregnant.* **Brian (21)** *is dressing for work, spliff in his mouth.*

Kathy (20) (*as she enters*) – **really goin' out** like that?

Brian (21) Just try n' stop me. Good trousers these, Kath.

Kathy Well I doubt they'll want yer servin' customers lookin' like the Grateful Dead.

Brian Then I'll take it up with the Union. Courdroy discrimination, it's a national scandal.

Kathy Scandal if they let yer through the door more like. Yer know it's gone half past.

Brian Don't worry, Mr Punctuality, me.

Kathy Yer said that about Woolworths.

Brian I could say a lot about them backstabbin' bastards.

Kathy 'Ow d'yer know British Home Stores are any different?

Brian 'Cause the Super's a Marxist, and they have coloureds on the tills. And they let yer go the pub on yer lunchbreak.

Kathy At least someone's havin' fun.

Brian Responsibilities, Kath. House int goin' to pay for itself.

Kathy This freezin' cold dump, yer mean. Flippin' toilet were frozen over when I went forra pee just now. Big cloud o'steam between me legs. I mean I knew rents were cheap up Burngreave, but I dint expect dark ages.

Brian Well all yer Pakistanis and Sikhs seem to like it, and at least I'm not goin' to get my 'ead kicked in for havin' long hair.

Kathy Were better off at my mum's. Pitsmoor by name, Pitsmoor by nature. Some dead old woman's junk everywhere still.

Brian Oh, I dunno – this thing's got some life left in it, look.

Brian *picks up and tries to tune the vintage radio from the previous owner.*

Static, the sound of BBC Radio Sheffield, playing "Whiter Shade of Pale" by Procul Harem.

Brian Bit of Tony Capstick t'get yer in the mood?

Kathy *grabs the radio and turns it off.*

Kathy Yer not funny.

Brian Oh, I'm deadly serious I am, Kath. (*Passes the spliff to* **Kathy**.) Hurdy Gurdy.

Kathy (*taking the spliff*) Hurdy Gurdy Hurdy Gurdy.

Kathy *takes a drag of the spliff.*

Should do that top button up, they'll only hold it against yer.

Spliff in mouth, **Kathy** *buttons up* **Brian***'s top button, straightening his white tie.*

Kathy Yer know I quite fancy you in a tie. Cute little baby-face.

Brian I'll 'ave you know this cute little baby-face were hitch-hikin' down Droitwich Free Festival when you were still arsin' around at school. John Mayall's Bluesbreakers in the pissin' rain. Me n'Sean n'a pocket full of quaaludes.

Kathy (*passes the spliff back*) Nursin' college, not school.

Brian Eh?

Kathy USH Nursin' College, and I certainly weren't arsin' around. You try changin' some dirty old sod's colostomy bag at the end of a twelve hour shift.

Brian Then it's a good job I came to yer rescue then, int it. The most beautiful girl this side o'Sheaf Market.

Kathy Mm, n' one split rubber johnny later I'm about as big as Sheaf Market. Twenty goin' on forty. Flower power on hold.

Brian On hold? Pfft, I'm fightin' capitalism from within, me.

Kathy Where, at British bloody Home Stores?

Brian Oh aye, John Lennon's got nothin' on me, babe. (*Sings, dances badly to make* **Kathy** *laugh.*) "Power to the People! Power to the People right on!" – 'Ere . . . –

Brian *escorts her to the armchair, placing a Littlewoods catalogue on her lap.*

Brian (*cont.*) – stop yer moanin', Yoko, have a look through that Littlewoods catalogue, see if there's a colour telly goin' cheap. Washin' machine or somert.

Kathy Don't need a washin' machine when I've got this one. He's doin' somersaults, feel.

Brian Oh . . . –

Kathy (*to her belly*) Spinnin' round like a little bloody acrobat aren't yer, love? Feel, go on.

Brian Yeah, no –

Kathy *places* **Brian**'*s hand on her belly.*

Kathy Can't yer feel it?

Brian No, it's proper good that, Kath. (*Passes her the spliff.*) Hurdy Gurdy.

Kathy (*takes the spliff*) Hurdy Gurdy, aye, yer know I might pop next door later, say hello to the neighbours.

Brian Well I hope yer've brushed up on yer Urdu. – 'Ey, don't worry about that mess, I reckon the rag n'bone man'll take most of it on Sunday, n'I'll call the coal-man t'drop off some fresh tomorrow. Get that fire goin', make it cosy for yer.

Brian *grabs his keys and kisses* **Kathy**.

Brian And if yer do us a Fray Bentos tonight, I'll bring yer back a Cherry B.

Brian *exits.*

Brian (*off*) Couple o'pints round the Bay Horse before closin'.

Kathy (*her stomach hurting, putting down the spliff*) Yeah, no, um . . .

Brian (*off*) Big company BHS, got to celebrate somehow. Never know, give it another year I might **be earnin' close to . . . –**

1971

Monday February 15th (Evening)

Brian (22) *enters with a bag of fish and chips and a handfull of loose change.* **Kathy (21)** *is on the sofa, feeding* **Baby Mike** *a bottle of formula.*

Brian (22) (*enters*) **– one n' nine** it says on the board. Give 'im two bob n'e refuses to take it. I'm like "says it on the board there, Des, one n'nine. Decimise yer own prices before yer start havin' a go at me".

He drops the loose change on the table.

Brian (22) Took us about half hour t'work out the soddin' change n'all. Fourteen new pennies when it's supposed to be two n' one, robbin' bastard.

Kathy (21) Who's a robbin' bastard?

Brian Chippy Des round the back. Doesn't even feel like real money, feel the weight.

Kathy Well, we'll just have to get used to it I s'ppose. Money's money.

Brian Yeah, and that's precisely why they'll never be a revolution in this country. 'Money's money.' Imagine if they took away the Deutschmark, eh? There'd be riots in Italy if they decimilised the lire, and yer can forget about Northern France. Pocket full o'half crowns I can't use.

Kathy Take 'em down the bank before yer go in tomorrow then, can't yer? Get 'em changed.

Brian We're on strike tomorrow, I told you that last night – don't look at me like that, I told yer.

Kathy You were better off at British Home Stores.

Brian Oh gi'oer, Kath, I'm wasted on a shop-floor, we're fightin' corruption on a massive scale, 'ere.

Kathy How about bein' skint on a massive scale? His nappies don't grow on trees, yer know.

Brian We'll be a lot worse off if the Government don't pay us our due.

Kathy Pay us whose due? Yerra part-time van driver for the GPO.

Brian Yeah, n'I'm still on the pay-roll, the Union – 'ey, we're in this together, aren't we? Someone's got to stand up for pretty young whats-'er-face at Pond Street sortin' office.

Kathy Who's pretty young whats-'er-face?

Brian It's a figure of speech. – Christ, yer startin' t' sound like me dad. Sat there, refusin' to see the bigger picture –

Kathy Well, he turned out alright dint 'e?

Brian Oh aye, run ragged down Steel Peach n' Tozers his whole life, bent over that furnace gobbin' up clots. It's blokes like 'im were up against, Kath. Too fuckin' weak n' subservient to stand up t'the management when it matters. Did yer bring the cutlery up?

Kathy No, the forks are demandin' overtime.

Brian Funny, yeah –

Kathy Yeah.

Brian Funny as this – (*Of Monty Python on the TV.*) . . . whatever the hell it's supposed to be. Dead parrot.

Kathy Could've been on a regular wage meself now.

Brian *opens the fish and chips with his hands.*

Kathy Brian –

Brian That's too much milk for a one-year-old I reckon.

Kathy It's formula. Busola lent it us.

Brian Who?

Kathy Busola next door, swears by it apparently. She's got three young 'uns of 'er own. Plus, it really soddin'-well hurts whenever I feed 'er like the . . . –

Brian Battered sausage.

Kathy What?

Brian Battered sausage. They only 'ad one cod, so I got us a battered sausage.

Beat.

Suit yerself.

Brian *bites into the battered sausage.*

Course, they'll probably have us back in on Wednesday anyway.

Kathy Best keep me fingers crossed then.

Brian No, but, yer know? Make a day of now can't we? Tomorrow, I mean. Take these down the bank like yer said. Make up for lost time if that's what yer want.

Kathy If that's what *I* want?

Brian Yeah, lost time, Kath, me n' you, um . . . The three of us like.

The **Baby** *makes gurgling noises.*

Brian See? Even short arse agrees with me, look. Get Sean n' Jules over, few drinks, few what-yer-ma-call-its. Beats sittin' in front of this crap every night, **could have a right bloody . . . –**

1972

<u>Sunday May 28th (Night)</u>

A party. **Brian (23)** *and* **Sean (24)** *have guitars and drinks.* **Kathy (22)** *and* **Jules** *have spliffs and drinks.*

Brian (23) **– . . . point of it, he doesn't have to answer to anyone.**

Sean (24) 'New Morning' is a piece of shit, Brian, the sooner you stop kidding yourself . . . –

Brian It's called re-invention.

Sean Oh Jesus, you are so fucking deluded.

Brian It's a great album.

Sean 'Blonde on Blonde's' a great album and that was five fucking years ago. Dylan's finished.

Brian I'm telling you it's a great album.

Sean 'Great album', there's only three decent tracks.

Brian 'Sign on the Window', 'Father of Night'.

Sean Over-produced granny music. He should leave that sort of shit to John Lennon.

Jules (24) **– . . . paddyfield thousands of miles from home,** except they shouldn't be out there in the first place.

Kathy (22) In the first place, yeah . . . –

Jules And he knows that more than anyone – Tricky Dicky . . . –

Kathy Tricky Dicky!

Jules Course he'll never come out and say they've surrendered.

Kathy Is he queer, do you think?

Jules Who, Richard Nixon? I wouldn't've thought he's anythin'. Someone who sends young men to Vietnam for no reason dunt deserve to be anythin'.

Kathy Looks nice, Vietnam. Nice trees.

Jules Nice or not, we'd be a lot better off if we did away with the libido altogether.

Kathy Did away, where's the fun in that?

Brian John Lennon wrote 'Norwegian Wood', Sean, he can produce as many grannies as he wants.

Sean Give me the Stones any day of the week.

Brian Hangin' off the coat-tails of the Beatles when they aren't rippin' off Robert Johnson.

Sean Alright, so let's talk about Hendrix if yer want to start stickin' the boot in.

Brian David Bowie.

Sean Ah, fuck off Bowie, that kid can't decide if he wants to be Syd Barrett or Lou Reed. Give me some actual fucking . . . –

Sean *picks up his guitar, strumming.*

Sean – . . . rock and roll, you know what I mean?

Brian Jim Morrison, Janis Joplin –

Sean Sure, if the stupid bastards hadn't both fucking croaked.

Brian Trout Mask Replica.

Sean Now Beefheart I don't mind.

Jules Now, if Richard Nixon had a vasectomy, –

Kathy Edward Heath.

Jules Edward Heath *is* a vasectomy. What we need is a female prime minister.

Kathy Yes!

Jules A woman with some actual fucking –

Kathy Tits!

Jules (*laughs*) Eh?

Kathy A woman with some actual tits!

Jules I was goin' to say balls.

Kathy Tits, balls – what's the difference? . . . – (*Spills wine on herself and the floor.*) Oh crap, all over my good clean top.

Jules The difference is centuries of misogyny and male-dominated patriarchy. If it were up to me I'd give 'em all the chop. Read yer Germaine Greer, it's time we burnt the bra.

Kathy I'm not burnin' my bra, this was two pounds fifty from Atkinsons.

Brian Country Joe n' the Fish!

Sean Ah, well now you're talking . . .

***Sean** sings and plays VERSE 1 of "Feel-Like-I'm-Fixin'-to-Die Rag" by Country Joe and the Fish.*

***Brian** joins in the song's chorus – singing/playing.*

Jules Should be compulsory, like gettin' the chop.

Kathy Gettin' the chop? D'yer know how many hospital beds that'd take?

Jules Yeah, well, if a bloke can't control himself after a few pints of John Smith's. If women like you end up throwin' a whole career away then it just means more work for the rest of us. Funny, I always thought Brian'd end up with someone older, more independent. Course, if yer end up up the duff, you end up up the duff, we can't all be Gloria Steinem.

***Kathy** moves to the boys and joins in singing the chorus of "Feel-Like-I'm-Fixin'-to-Die Rag" by Country Joe.*

***Jules** joins **Kathy, Sean** and **Brian** sing the FINAL LINE OF THE CHORUS, and they cheer/ laugh, with –*

Sean Mamas and the Papas eat your heart out! We should take over King Mojo's.

Jules Ha, Penny Farthing more like.

Kathy 'Ere, play Kathy's Song, Sean!

Brian Fuckin' Fitzalan Square.

Sean I'm serious, Brian, screw all this happy families bollocks. How / about we put the band back together? –

Kathy / Kathy's Song, Kathy's Song! Come on, yer know yer love me, you big . . .

Kathy *drapes herself over* **Sean**.

Kathy . . . sexy Irish troubadour, you.

Jules Alright, steady on, Kath . . . –

Sean No no, you carry on, Kathy, . . .

Kathy Jules reckons I should burn my bra.

Sean Get upstairs, I'll bring the matches.

Jules *moves to* **Brian**, *passing him a joint.*

Jules (*as she does so*) Well, the heart wants what the heart wants.

Brian Ha, you made your bed quick enough. So much for free love. 'Ere, how about this for an encore?

Brian ***strikes his guitar and starts playing/singing Helen Reddy's "I Am Woman".***

After the first four lines of the first verse, he moves straight into the big triumphant chorus, and –

Kathy, **Jules** *and* **Sean** *laugh, jump to their feet and join in.*

As they reach the final word of the chorus, the scene instantly snaps to –

1972

Monday May 29th (Daytime)

Kathy (23) *and* **Mike (2)** *sit on the sofa watching 'Play School' on the black and white TV.*

Kathy (*with the TV*) **– . . . a house**,
Here's a door,
Windows –
One, two, three, four,
Ready to knock,
Turn the lock, it's –

She watches a bit more of Play School, stroking **Mike**'*s hair.*

Kathy (23) (*with the TV*) Humpty, Hamble n' Big Ted.

Mike (2) Ted Ted.

Kathy (*with the TV*) Little Ted, Jemima, Big Ted . . .–

Mike Big Ted.

Kathy (*to* **Mike**, *strokes his hair*) It is Big Ted, yer right. Clever boy.

Mike Big Ted.

Mike *yawns, dozes off.* **Kathy** *discreetly reaches over for her spliff from the ashtray.*

As she lights the spliff –

Kathy Big Ted, Little Ted, Humpty, **Hamble, Dapple n' –**

Suddenly, there's a blackout.

Kathy **– Bollocks.**

Brian (24) Well, I did warn yer.

Kathy I thought they said the blackouts weren't till ten o'clock.

Brian It is ten o'clock, mind yer arse.

Kathy Ow!

Brian Mind yer flippin' . . . –

1973

<u>Friday December 14th (Evening)</u>

In the darkness, **Brian (24)** *is holding a couple of candles, looking for somewhere to put them.*

Kathy (23) *is laying on the sofa, smoking a spliff, holding a copy Germaine Greer's* The Female Eunuch.

They both giggle.

Kathy (23) You mind your arse, I bet all your bastard Union chiefs aren't sat round in the dark.

Brian (24) Aye, n'neither's Ted Heath, but if it's what it takes to improve our wages then they can turn the power off all week as far as I'm concerned.

Kathy Need a job first, Bri.

Brian I have got a job. Rhythm guitar and harmonies, Sean on lead.

Kathy A proper job, he's goin' to turn four next year. –

Brian Thousands of proper jobs, Kathy, aye, yer know what I mean. I doubt Clapton's pluggin' in his Fender tonight, either.

He finally lights the candles as **Kathy** *takes her copy of Germaine Greer's* Female Eunuch *and tries to read.*

Brian Reckon he'll stay down like?

Kathy Guess as long as the curtains don't go up in flames.

Brian Cards or Scrabble?

Kathy Neither.

Kathy *passes the spliff to* **Brian**.

Kathy (*as she does so*) Says here I'm the unpaid employee of the heterosexual male.

Brian Who?

Kathy Well, that's what it says here. Book Jules lent us. "A housewife's work has no results. Bringin' up children is not a real occupation. The housewife is the unpaid employee of the heterosexual male."

Brian Best get me wallet then.

Kathy Well, I wunt want to deprive yer of yer pools' money.

Brian Ooh cuttin', yeah –

Kathy: Should ask Val at the post office if they'll 'ave yer back. Yer know, I've read the same sentence three times now?

Brian Must be a good sentence.

Kathy It is good, I could always finish my trainin'.

Brian What?

Kathy I said I could go back n'finish my trainin'. Nursin' school.

Brian Oh gi'over, yer not goin' / back t'that –

Kathy I'm twenty-three, I'm hardly kickin' / the bucket.

Brian You are not goin' back t'that dirty old Infirmary, Kath, no chance. Cleanin' up other people's crap? Thought yer'd done enough o'that when yer dad were laid out.

Kathy Cleaned up plenty o' your son's crap. Maybe yer should try it sometime, Bri –

Brian I'll kill bloody Jules.

Kathy Oh, bless, someone's not a fan of the female eunuch?

Brian Not unless they're prog rock. 'Ey, maybe I should stay 'ome n'do the ironin' while I'm at it n'all? Mop the / kitchen floor?

Kathy Take yer keks off, more like.

Brian Eh?

Kathy Take your shitty keks off, show us what yer made of.

Kathy *puts her book down.*

Kathy Reckon we've got a while before he needs his potty yet. Three minutes at least.

Brian Three minutes? Oh, gi'over . . . –

Kathy (*taking the spliff from* **Brian**) Hurdy Gurdy.

Brian What?

Kathy (*takes a quick drag*) Hurdy Gurdy Hurdy Gurdy . . . –

Kathy *quickly stubs out the spliff, then starts pulling down* **Brian***'s trousers and pants.*

Brian 'Ere, fuckin' 'ell . . . Christ, are you –?

They get undressed, quickly/clumsily.

Brian Hold on a minute then –

Kathy Lift yer arse up, shift. Mind yer foot.

Brian I'm doin' it, aren't I? You alright?

Kathy I'm alright, yeah. God bless the National Grid.

Brian God bless the three day week.

Kathy One day week round 'ere.

Brian Alright, rent-a-gob, yer don't 'ave to wind me up just 'cause I've got me willy out. **'Ere, just –**

1974

<u>Thursday September 5th (Evening)</u>

Brian (25) **– . . . stay calm, alright?** Taxi'll be here in a minute, they won't be takin' yer anywhere thrashin' about like that.

Kathy (24) I don't care, just get it out of 'ere, Bri – fuckin' uuuuUUUUR! Fuck fuckin' 'ell!

Brian 'Ere, sit up, get back on the/sofa . . . –

Kathy / You get back, yer twat.

Brian Alright, well wait till yer get t'the hospital at least. Can't 'ave it droppin' out all over the carpet –

Kathy (*hitting him*) Drop it on your head, this is your fuckin' fault!

Brian Alright alright, just . . . –

Brian *grabs the vinyl sleeve of "Dark Side of the Moon" and fans* **Kathy** *with it.*

Brian (*fanning her*) – . . . relax, Kathy, alright?

Kathy Stop wavin' that bloody Dark Side at me will yer?! – Uuur dear god, she's persistant.

Honking of a car horn from outside.

Brian That's the taxi now, look. – (*To* **Mike**.) Front door, Mike, do somert useful with yer life! – (*To* **Kathy**.) 'Ere, let's get yer up you.

Kathy God, it's too big. It's too big, Brian –

Brian (*laughs*) I know, that's what all the girls say.

Kathy *hits* **Brian**.

Brian Ow! Fuckin' hell, alright – (*Calls.*) Mike!

Kathy (*hitting him*) Yer think this is fuckin' funny, yer stupid hippy – (*Sudden contraction.*) Oh my god, uuuuuaaaaaarrrr!

The **Taxi Driver** *enters, followed by a tearful* **Mike**, *moving straight to* **Kathy**.

Brian Alright, yeah, we're just 'ere.

Taxi Driver Grab onto my shoulder, duck, that's it.

Mike (4) (*crying*) Is mummy going to die?

Brian People don't die, Michael, grow up. (*To* **Taxi Driver**.) 'Ere, I can do that mate . . . –

Taxi Driver No no, I've got 'er. (*To* **Mike**.) She'll be right as rain, son, don't worry. Goin' to 'ave a little brother or sister to take care of by mornin', eh? (*To* **Brian**.) Northern General?

Brian (*slipping the* **Taxi Driver** *a note*) / Keep the change, lad, yeah. (*To* **Kathy**.) He's going to drop yer by the main doors, alright? I've already called reception, they know yer on yer way.

The **Taxi Driver** *supports* **Kathy** *and leads her out, exiting.*

Mike *nervously watches on.*

Kathy (*as she goes*) Make sure he gets to nursery tomorrow, there's Ricicles in the top cupboard.

Brian (*takes* **Mike**'*s hand*) Alright, yeah. (*To* **Mike**.) You 'eard yer mother . . . –

Kathy (*in the hallway, off*) And spaghetti hoops for 'is tea. He likes his toast cut into soldiers.

Brian Soldiers, aye, we'll manage!

Sound of front door closing. **Brian** *cracks open a can of lager.*

Brian (*to* **Mike**) We'll manage forra night won't we, Private? –

Mike *thumps* **Brian**.

Mike You dead-ed her, stupid!

Mike *exits, running into the hallway after his mum.*

Brian – Well yer can forget about yer bloody Ricicles, morbid little shit. Flippin' well fend f'yersen f'once, see how far yer get. I **should let you –**

1975

Wednesday January 8th (Evening)

Brian (26) – **cry it out, she's** supposed to cry it out.

Kathy (25) (*off*) Cry it out till when? This time tomorrow?

Kathy *enters – wearing her nurse's uniform – holding a crying* **Baby Rebecca**.

Brian *flicks through Doctor Spock's* Common Sense Book of Baby and Childcare.

Brian Well, that's what Doctor Spock says. Page 56, look, it's underlined. "Put the baby to bed at a reasonable hour, say good night and don't go back."

As they speak, **Mike (5)** *enters, with a fizzy drink and a football sticker book. He sits on the floor and opens his brand new packs of stickers.*

Brian (*cont., reads*) "Do not reassure her that you are nearby. This only enrages her and keeps her crying much longer."

Kathy What a load of crap.

Brian Christ, I'm only sayin' what it says.

Kathy Alright, fine, you –

Kathy *hands* **Baby Rebecca** *to* **Brian**, *and exits into the hallway.*

Kathy (*exits, off*) – be my guest, Brian, I'm runnin' late as it is. My shift dunt finish till five in the mornin' n' the last thing I want's another fight before I go in.

Brian Who's fightin' with yer? –

Baby Rebecca *poos in her nappy.*

Brian Ooh, that's a stinker.

Baby Rebecca *giggles.*

Kathy (*off, cont.*) You are and I'm frazzled enough as it is. I've got to get in, change, go through the handover sheets –

Brian No, I'm sure I'm sure. (*To* **Rebecca**.) We're sure aren't we, Rebecca?

Brian, *carrying* **Baby Rebecca**, *moves into the hallway, exits.*

Brian (*to* **Kathy**, *off*) – 'Ear that, Kath? She says don't you worry, mum! Me n' 'er, **we're goin' to be –**

1975

Thursday 5th June (Evening)

Brian (26) *enters from the hall, singing and playing guitar – a silly song.*

He is followed by **Rebecca (1)** *learning to walk by cruising along the furniture with difficulty.*

Brian (*sings and plays*)
– having a walk on your own two feet,
Having a walk on your own two feet,
Having a walk on your own two trotters,
Having a walk on your
Own two hooves!

Rebecca *squeals, claps hands.* **Brian** *laughs, and kisses* **Rebecca**.

Brian (26) That's it, clever girl. Who's my thousand puddings, eh?

He gives her a hug, kisses her head.

There's my thousand puddings! Shall we give it another go?

Rebecca (1) Dada. Dada

Brian Dada Dada, yes. –

Mike (5) *enters with a fizzy drink, a football sticker book and a brand new pack of stickers.*

Brian (*cont., to* **Rebecca**) – Now can you say Lennon'? Say 'John Lennon'.

Mike 'Ere, Dad, I've got Ray Clemence finally. Dad –

Brian Football's for yobs, put on the telly n'learn somethin'.

Brian *switches on the TV – it's the BBC News reporting on the EEC Referendum.*

Brian I bet David Dimbleby never 'ad no sticker book when 'e were growin' up. (*To* **Rebecca**.) Say 'Common Market'. Shall we join the Common Market? Come on, darling.

Rebecca Da. Dada –

Brian *exits, followed by* **Rebecca**.

Rebecca Dada, Dad . . . –

Mike Ray Clemence, look. 'E's like the best goalie in the world. I mean, that's what Hanif sez and Hanif's got every sticker in every book of last two seasons. So this is Ray Clemence n' that's Emlyn Hughes. There's Alan Ball n' Kevin Keegan with the funny hair **n' this one's –**

Enter **Hanif (6)**, *with a football.*

1976

<u>Saturday August 14th (Day)</u>

There's a summer heatwave.

"Save All Your Kisses" by Brotherhood of Man on the radio.

Hanif (6) (*as he enters*) – **Charlie George,** yer spaz!

Mike – Who you callin' spaz?! You're the spakker. Hanif!

Hanif *lobs the ball at* **Mike**, *who misses it.*

Hanif (6) (*laughs*) Some Peter Shilton! More like Giant Haystacks!

Mike (6) That's 'cause I'm striker, Hanif! You be goalie for once!

Mike *lobs the ball back at* **Hanif**.

Laughing, they dangerously lob the ball back at each other, and . . .

Rebecca (2) *enters, in a pretty outfit, holding Sooty and Sweep toys.*

She sings/dances along to "Save All Your Kisses for Me" – replacing the word baby for Hanif – as **Mike** *and* **Hanif** *chuck/kick the ball around.*

Rebecca *tries to kiss* **Mike** *on the cheek as part of her routine.*

Mike – *annoyed – pushes* **Rebecca** *over, who lands on the floor –*

Hanif Oh naow, Mike!

Mike Shuddup, it weren't me!

Rebecca (2) (*crying*) Daddeeeeeeee!!!! –

Mike *rushes to grab and hide the ball,* **Hanif** *helps* **Rebecca** *up, as –*

Brian (27) – *wearing an apron with nothing but his Y-fronts underneath – enters, carrying* **Rebecca**'*s bowl of slushy Weetabix and a can of lager.*

Rebecca Daddeeeeeeeee!!

Brian (27) (*on entering*) The 'ell 'ave you done to 'er this time?! Abbeyfield Park too good f'yer, is it?

Hanif It weren't me, it were Mike!

Rebecca He hit arm, look! Mike!

Mike Oh gi'oer, don't lie!

Brian *clips* **Mike** *round the head, making* **Hanif** *laugh.*

Mike Ow! – Alright Hanif, it int funny –

Brian No, it int funny, Mike, runnin' round like a pair o'bloody puffters in the middle of a heatwave. Need to cool you both off I reckon.

Brian *sprays his can of lager at* **Mike** *and* **Hanif**.

They laugh.

Brian – 'Ere . . . –

Brian *removes a note from his apron pocket and gives it to* **Mike**.

Brian Run round Mr Kings n' get me a couple cans of Whitbread for later. Don't tell yer mum – or tell 'er, I don't know, god knows what time she'll be home. (*To* **Hanif**.) You – not a word to your weirdo parents.

Mike (*pockets the money*) Can we get Vampire lollies, then?

Hanif Yeah, can we get Vampire lollies, Mike's dad, please?

Brian Yeah, if yer must, take yer sister with yer. Good f'you I got –

Hanif *grabs* **Rebecca**'*s hand, and* **Rebecca**, **Mike** *and* **Hanif** *dart out the living room, exiting.*

Brian (*cont.*) – my giro today. – (*Calls after him.*) 'Ey, and if Derek won't serve yer the Whitbread tell 'im Brian sent yer! – (*Sees a neighbour.*) Yeah, you n'all, Mrs Gorman, thanks!

Enjoyin' the heatwave are yer, love? (**Brian** *remembers he's only got his Y-fronts on under the apron.*) Well, yer've got to make the most of what yer've got, that's what me wife always says! I said yer've got t'make the **most of what yer . . . –**

Kathy (27) **– . . . got no roof over our heads** if yer keep pissin' yer giro away on booze. Where's the rent book?

Brian (28) I don't know, somewhere.

Kathy *yanks the rent book from* **Brian**'*s apron pocket.*

1977

<u>Thursday December 1st (Evening)</u>

Kathy'*s just home from work, in her nurse's uniform.* **Brian**'*s very drunk.*

Brian Christ, it's like livin' under the Stasi wi'you sometimes.

Kathy *leafs through the rent book.*

Brian Look, they're meant to be givin' us a rebate aren't they? I've told yer, I've got it / covered.

Kathy / Five weeks without a stamp. That's what yer call covered is it?

Brian Alright, I know it looks bad . . . –

Kathy Five weeks fuckin' rent owed. Don't click yer fingers at me –

Brian Just give it 'ere a minute, I told yer I've got it under / control.

Kathy / Three bob ten a week, that's close to twenty pounds we owe them now.

Brian Oh it's alright, they don't care –

Kathy Course they care, this is Council property. What if they take us to court, eh?

Beat.

Kathy Brian –

Brian Well, they'd have to send an Housin' Officer to investigate first.

Kathy Oh, that's alright then. For all I fuckin' know, they've already been several times already. Flat on yer back, pissed all day –

Brian I'm not flat on my back, it goes Housin' Officer then Court and even then they might still give us a rebate. Besides, I'm lookin' after Rebecca, aren't I? Fuckin' pickin' up Mike every day after school –

Kathy Oh, right, and I've got all the time in the world 'ant I? Six shifts a week, twenty odd patients to look after every night.

Brian Yeah, and this is what you wanted, Kath, remember? Equality! Women's Lib n'all that, it's not my fault yer tired. Bunch o'lesbians marchin' up n' down Trafalgar Square with their bras in the air? Solves nothin', absolutely nothin'.

Kathy *death-stares.*

Brian Look, I'll take it down first thing if yer worried.

Kathy I am worried. I'm worried yer goin' to 'ave us turfed out by Christmas.

Brian Okay, so I'll pay it off then, get yer precious stamps –

Kathy What with? Yer goin' to go buskin' down the Hole in the Road again? You n' Sean like a shit Simon n'Garfunkel. More like The Barron Knights.

Brian We weren't that bad.

Kathy You were a laughin' stock, even the fish keeled over. For Christ's sake, someone's got to pay the rent and I'm only on twelve pound a week, that's less than you get signin' on. –

As **Kathy** *speaks,* **Rebecca (3)** *enters, dressed and made-up like a punk. Stands in the doorway, watching on.*

Kathy (*cont.*) – Three bob for the rent, two pound fifty for the gas, another pound on top of that for the coal. Food in the cupboard, the kids –

Brian Don't worry about the kids, I'll take care of the kids.

Rebecca (3) My name's Rotten.

Brian *bursts out laughing.*

Rebecca (*jumps up and down*) Rotten Rotten Rotten Rotten.

Kathy Oh for fucksake –

Brian (*laughs*) Oh come on! Come on, Kath, it's called fun or somert. (*Sings.*) "No woman no cry. No woman –"

Kathy No woman no fuck off.

Kathy *grabs* **Brian***'s can of lager and necks it.*

Brian 'Ey alright, careful –

Rebecca Mummy spillin'!

Kathy *hurls the can across the room, and . . .*

Brian (*to* **Rebecca**) Back upstairs, go on. (*Calls up.*) Mike, help yer sister wash 'er face!

Rebecca *exits.* **Kathy** *moves to the sideboard, taking a handful of coins from the glass jar.*

Brian Flippin' 'ell, Kath, yer frightenin' the kids. Yer realise that money's meant for the lekky meter?

Kathy I don't care, I'm goin' Mucky Duck.

Brian What?

Kathy I'm goin' the Mucky Duck, Jules invited me to the Mucky Duck tonight. I wasn't goin' to mention it 'cause I thought . . . like an idiot I actually thought it wouldn't be fair on you –

Brian What, at this time? But you haven't even cooked tea yet.

Kathy Cabaret Voltaire are playin'.

Brian Who?

Kathy Cabaret Voltaire – Don't look at me like that, I've got no fuckin' idea who they are either, yer can friggin' well –

She puts her coat back on, and exits.

Kathy (*cont., as she exits*) – give yer brother a ring if it's money yer need.

Brian My brother? Don't talk daft, 'e's even more stuck-up than you! Just imagine what 'e'd say if 'e walked in 'ere right now, **'e'd say –**

Geoff (30) **– yer a tosspot, Brian, end of.** Are yer tellin' me yer wouldn't want a decent salary n' a company car?

Brian (28) I'm not comin' to work for yer.

Geoff Trips down the smoke, a holiday abroad every year? Damn sight better than sittin' on yer arse, pickin' at yer dangleberries fifty-two weeks a year.

Brian Look, yer can waffle on all yer like, Geoff –

1977

Sunday December 25th
<u>(Christmas Day)</u>

Brian (28) *and brother* **Geoff (30)**, *wearing Christmas cracker hats – drinking and smoking.*

Noise of kids from the other room. Christmas Top of the Pops on the black and white telly – The Wombles "Wombling Merry Christmas".

Geoff (30) Waffle on? I'm offerin' you way out, skid-mark. There's blokes who'd bite my knob off for a job at our firm. Qualified, hard-workin' grafters –,

Brian So what yer wastin' yer breath on me for then?

Geoff Oh I dunno, to save your marriage? Because yer my younger brother and I love yer?

Brian Alright, Don Vito, easy on the Three Barrels.

Geoff It's Hennessy, bellend. And if yer think there's no decent work around now, yer goin' to be in for one hell of a surprise in a year or two. Things gettin' cheaper, people buyin' n' sellin' from all over the world.

Brian Well I'm not buyin' n' sellin' all over world.

Geoff No, because yer've got the Internationals comin' in n' sortin' out the mess that yer precious Trade Unions made. Blame yer mate Harold Wilson for takin' us into the

Common Market, the days of coalmines n'butchers shops are over. Have yer been to the new Asda up Handsworth yet? It's like Battlestar Galactica.

Mike (7) *enters, wielding his toy light-sabre.*

Mike (7) (*as he enters*) Feel the power of the force! Feel the power of Vadar!

Over the next, **Mike** *practices moves with his lightsabre, as* **Brian** *and* **Geoff** *continue talking.*

Geoff Look, just think about it, alright? The commercial timber trade is thrivin' right now. We've got business all over Germany, South America . . . –

Brian Yeah, n'if yer think I'm goin' to spend the rest of my life choppin' down the rainforest.

Geoff Gi'over 'rainforest', yer'd be in the office with me.

Brian What, as your tea-boy?

Geoff No, dickhead, yer'd be helpin' me run the place. I'm regional manager, you'd be my deputy.

Brian (*laughs*) Yeah, right –

Geoff Yeah right, 'cause you'd turn down three-and-a-half grand a year. Happier bein' an housewife, stoned out your mind, beggin' on the phone to me or dad everytime yer dole-money runs out. Stuck in Burngreave with all yer Paki's everywhere.

Rebecca (3) *enters, wearing a sari – and with a bindi on her forehead.*

Rebecca (3) Bindi, Uncle Geoff, it's your turn now. Mrs Patel from two doors down give us bindis and now everyone has to have a bindi! You too, Daddy!

As **Geoff** *and* **Brian** *speak,* **Rebecca** *places stick-on bindis on their foreheads, as –*

Brian Can't say they bother me, Geoff. People are people.

Geoff Not on the property market they're not. Wait till Mrs Thatcher's in Downin' Street, she'll turn an area like this upside down – have yer not heard of the Right to Buy? Do the right thing n' yer'll be able to buy this place off Council in a year or two. Big old Victorian refurb like this, yer could split it up into bedsits if yer want. Charge yer coloureds whatever yer want n'yer move out to Grenoside near me n'Gayle.

Brian And a happy Christmas to you n'all, Geoff, I think I'd rather pull me teeth out.

Brian *moves/sits, busying himself opening the board game Mastermind.*

Geoff *joins him, eyeing up Top of the Pops on the TV.*

Geoff What d'yer make of ABBA, Bri?

Brian Well, I'd give the blonde one a go.

Geoff More of a Pan's People man, mesen.

Mike *whacks* **Rebecca** *with the sabre, offstage.*

Aunty Gayle (33), *followed by* **Kathy**, *enter.*

Aunty Gayle (33) Arrr, there she is, look! Our very own Indian princess!

Aunty Gayle *places her Christmas cracker-crown on* **Rebecca***'s head and sings along to the "Wombling Merry Christmas".*

Aunty Gayle *and* **Rebecca** *hold hands and dance/sing –* **Kathy** *joins in.*

Mike *doesn't.*

Gayle, Rebecca *and* **Kathy** *sing the final line of the chorus – and cheer/laugh.*

Mike Stupid Wombles, no one likes the Wombles.

Rebecca No one likes *Star Wars*!

Mike *chases* **Rebecca** *with his light-sabre. They exit, as . . .*

Aunty Gayle Arr, we we should spend Christmas together every year. – Oh, I almost forgot . . .

Aunty Gayle *finds a wrapped present from the side and hands to* **Kathy**.

Aunty Gayle (*as she does so*) Mind the Sellotape, that's

Rebecca (*off*) Ow! Daddeee!

Brian *looks to* **Kathy**.

Brian (*to* **Kathy**) I'll go shall I? (*To* **Geoff**.) Yer see what I 'ave to put up with?

Brian *exits, leaving* **Geoff** *to open the Mastermind game on his own.*

Rackham's own paper is that. I'm thrilled Mike liked his light-sabre.

Kathy *unwraps the present.*

Aunty Gayle Yer know they'd nearly all sold out of 'em at Redgates.

Kathy Oh –

Kathy *has opened the present. It's a fancy cushioned box, with a cutlery set inside.*

– god, you really didn't have to.

Aunty Gayle Nice that it comes in its own display box, int it? Cushioned.

Kathy No yeah, it's . . . –

Kathy *opens the lid, reveals the cutlery set.*

Cutlery, thank you. (*To* **Geoff**.) Thank you –

Geoff Well, she likes it, I haven't got a clue.

Aunty Gayle Those in the know say it'll double in price in a few year. We saw it advertised in the Sunday Times supplement dint we, Geoff? Nana Mousouri swears by it. Honestly, Kathy, sometimes you just say t'yerself 'what the hell' –

Geoff 'What the hell', Gayle, aye – you only go round once. And if Brian pulls 'is 'ead out of arse, then this time next year – who knows, right? For all we know, there **might be . . . –**

Kathy (28) (*calls to* **Brian**) – **. . . a rat!** There's another bloody rat under the tree!

1978

Monday December 25th (Christmas Day)

She moves to the living room doorway.

Kathy (28) (*calls*) Brian? I thought I told yer to take the rubbish out last night!

Brian (29) (*off*) Alright, I'm doin' it, fuckin' 'ell –

Brian *enters, covered in snow from outside, holding three or four stuffed bin-bags.*

Brian (*as he enters*) – give me a second n'I'll chase it out with the others. I'll get Mike out of bed, he'll want to open 'is stockin' anyway.

Kathy Yeah, if 'is selection box hasn't already been chewed up.

As she speaks, **Kathy** *quickly changes into her uniform.*

Kathy (*cont.*) Maybe don't leave dirty plates everywhere instead of puttin' 'em in the sink.

Brian Yeah, and there's about ten bin bags out the front already.

Kathy So? I'm not havin' the kids get sick again 'cause you can't be bothered –

Brian I am fuckin' bothered! (*Tones it down.*) I am bothered, Kath – Look, just . . .

He starts ushering **Kathy** *out of the room.*

Rebecca (*off*) Catch him, catch him, Mike! Get 'im some biccies n'cheese!

Brian – clear off n' let me deal with it. Aren't yer meant to be on the ward by now anyway? Yer know, some might call you a scab, whole country / on strike.

Kathy / Get lost will yer 'scab'? It's 'life n' limb cover', there's kids who haven't been out of bed for months. Tiny little kids with –

Brian Leukemia, yeah, yer said. 'Ere, take these –

Brian *hands the bin-bags to* **Kathy**.

Brian – with yer on the way out. Don't worry, I'll save yer some turkey **n' I'll tell the kids yer –**

1979

Friday February 2nd (Afternoon)

Brian (30) (*on phone*) – **sorry, Dad, I know. No, I know** yer ashamed, no one's more ashamed than than me . . . Anythin' really, few quid. Five pounds so I can pay the rent off, I'm . . . here on my own now Rebecca's at nursery, I'm – (*Hits himself over the head with the phone.*) Fuckin' tryin', aren't I? . . . Music for fucksake, freedom. Freedom to live like real . . . Like individuals, Dad! – yeah, I know . . . I know that, I know. I know I've got to start **livin' in the –**

1979

Thursday May 3rd (Late Evening)

The General Election results are on television. **Brian (30)**, **Jules (31)** *and* **Sean (31)** *are smoking, drinking.* **Sean** *and* **Brian** *have their guitars.*

Jules (31) – **. . . real world after Callaghan thought he could** take on the Tories and win.

Sean (31) Then they should've listened to Tony Benn and put a real leader in charge.

Jules How d'yer know Thatcher's not a real leader? Because she's a woman?

Sean (31) Hey, I don't care what she's got hidden in her knickers as long as she doesn't screw over the rest of us.

Jules (31) It matters to me.

Sean Of course it matters to you, you're a feminist – your whole ideology is based on the assumption that women are victims and that's as dangerous and dehumanising as Page 3.

Jules Arr, thanks for putting me straight, Sean –

Sean You're welcome. If there's one thing I know it's that sexual politics shouldn't mix with politics, it's just like religion – the fucking Ayotollah or whoever.

Jules Sinn Féin.

Sean There's nothing sexual about those mad cunts, at least the Ayotollah wears a dress.

Jules (*imitates Ian Paisley*) "We will never apologise, no!"

Sean And since when was Ian Paisley from the West Indies? Fucking Mike Yarwood here –

Brian (30) It's just the same old shit. Wilson, Callaghan, Thatcher –

Sean If only it was the same old shit. We're witnessing the death of socialism here –

Jules Oh, please, like we've ever really had socialism.

Sean You want a real leader? Give me Clement Attlee or Nye Bevin –

Jules Adolf Hitler.

Sean Well, if it's Nationalism yer want, then Maggie's your man.

Brian She's not my man.

Sean Kathy's your man, Bri, we all know that.

Brian (*picks up guitar*) Yeah, and some of us haven't quite given up on the sixties just yet.

Brian ***starts singing/ playing "Age of Aquarius" by Fifth Dimension on his guitar.***

Sean Ha, I gave up on the sixties after Altamont. If Woodstock had worked then I wouldn't be sweeping the floor of Tinsley steelworks, coming home covered in asbestos every night –

Brian Neil Young's still got it, Joni Mitchell. Lennon n' McCartney . . . –

Sean Of course they've still got it, they're millionaires.

Jules I just want to get pissed.

Sean Amen

Jules Amen indeed –

Sean *and* **Jules** *clink their drinks and kiss.*

Jules To the end of days.

Sean To the end of your arse, read yer Nostradamus. "Yea, the devil in a blue fucking dress."

Jules Yea, with a voice like **nails on blackboard n' a face like –**

1980

Tuesday December 9th (Late Evening)

The News is on. **Kathy** *arrives from work with fish and chips.*

Kathy (30) (*as she enters*) **– . . . mushy peas by accident, look.** Accidently on purpose maybe, one of the two. Either way, yer'll have to make do, I'm not walkin' all the way round the back again now.

Kathy *unwraps the fish and chips.* **Brian (31)** *stares at the television.*

Pause.

Kathy Yer goin' to sit there with a face-on all night?

Pause. She continues.

Whatever, Brian, I'm used to it by now.

Pause. She continues.

Terry at work. Yer remember Terry, don't yer? Senior Porter, he met us at East House that time. You were shit-faced I think.

Pause. She continues.

Kathy Well, Terry kindly asked me if I wanted to go see *Ordinary People* on Friday. *Ordinary People* – the Robert Redford thing, it's on at the ABC. Friday night after work, yer don't mind if I keep 'im company, do yer? Poor thing just went through a messy divorce with his wife. Either that or he's bent, I haven't quite worked 'im out yet.

Pause.

Brian.

Pause.

Suit yerself, I don't care. Sit there cryin' into yer beer again.

Pause.

Brian . . .

Brian (31) Someone shot 'im, look.

Kathy What?

Brian Lennon.

Pause.

Some bastard shot John Lennon, look. Why'd they do that, eh, Kath? Why?

The news report is about John Lennon's murder outside the Dakota Building, New York.

Brian *turns the volume on the TV up.*

They watch.

Kathy Oh Brian, . . . –

Brian I need a drink. I need to . . . –

Brian *hesitates, then makes to get up and go –*

– . . . get out of here, I need to . . . –

Brian *grabs his things (cigarettes, keys).*

Kathy No, wait – what about yer fish n'chips?

Brian . . . see Geoff or somert.

Kathy Geoff? 'Ey, 'old on, yer can't just bugger off to yer brother's at this time of night.

Brian I fuckin' love you, yer know.

Kathy What?

He makes for the living room door.

Brian, please, **yer can't just . . .**

Mike *and* **Hanif** *burst in, in their school uniforms. They sing/mime/dance around to Adam and the Ants' "Stand and Deliver" on the radio.*

As they dance about, **Mike (11)** *grabs a bottle of gin from his parents' stash and the boys glug from it.*

1981

<u>Thursday May 7th (Afternoon)</u>

Hanif (11) *pulls out a packet of Benson and Hedges cigarettes, and they both try smoking for the first time.*

Mike (11) *makes to wretch, running out the living room, when . . .*

The door bursts open – the music changes to Bucks Fizz "Making Your Mind Up" – and . . .

Rebecca (7), *in school uniform, accompanied by two schoolfriends –* **Karen (11)** *and* **Nicole (11)** *rush in and perform a routine to the song, entertaining* **Mike** *and* **Hanif**.

Mike *and* **Hanif** *grab cushions from the sofa and start chasing/hitting the girls – turning into a massive pillow fight, when . . .*

The music changes to Human League "Don't You Want Me", and . . .

Kathy (31) – *dressed for work, but with a new hairdo – enters, spraying herself with perfume.*

The kids scatter as . . .

Brian (32) *enters, in his work-clothes, with a briefcase and a Charles and Diana mug of coffee.*

Brian (32) (*enters*) – **thought I'd go up Concorde Sports Centre straight after** work. Promised Geoff a couple o' games of squash. That alright?

Kathy (31) That's fine, Brian, yeah, yer Passport to Leisure's on the side.

Brian Looks like we're goin' to be stocktakin' again all day. Reckon I'll need to smack 'im about the court just to remind 'im what's what.

Kathy How very macho of yer.

Brian Macho as they come me. Got a swing like John McEnroe –

1981

<u>Friday May 7th (Morning)</u>

"Don't You Want Me" playing on the radio.

The black and white television has been replaced with a colour TV. There's a portable gas fire instead of the coal fire. A new sofa.

Brian *swings and pinches* **Kathy**'*s arse – as* **Mike (11)** *and* **Rebecca (7)** *enter, in school uniforms, with bowls of Sugar Puffs.*

Kathy Wish you had a perm like John McEnroe. Don't forget I'm pickin' up the Right to Buy form from Spital Hill housin' office straight after work so this one'll have to pick Rebecca up from school.

Mike I'll have to do what? Arr, gi'oer, I'm meant to be goin' over Hanif's to practice with 'is nunchucks! Honest, dad, they're proper Bruce Lee nunchucks from the Wicker!

Rebecca No flippin' way! Can't I just walk back with Keely n' Kirsty's mum? It's embarrassin' whenever 'e turns up. Stuffin' 'is face with Frazzles all the way 'ome.

Kathy (*to* **Brian**) Said I'd have a drink with Sean n'Jules at the East House after if yer fancy it?

Brian Take 'em over Sahib's on West Street, make a night of it. (*Hugs and kisses her.*) Little Queen Enema all grown up. Never thought we'd actually own this dump.

Kathy Splash of Dunhill?

Brian Splash of Dunhill.

Kathy *picks up and sprays Dunhill aftershave on* **Brian***'s neck.*

Brian Ooh, that's the stuff –

Mike Can't we come to Sahib's?

Brian You shut yer gob, D minus, yer can get yersen a fishcake from the chinky. That is unless yer want to take on me n' yer uncle at squash –

Mike Yeah right, int even real game. Only puffs play squash.

Brian (*camps it up*) Well, I'd best wear me lipstick then 'ant I, sailor?

Rebecca He's already put on mum's lipstick with Hanif once.

Mike 'Ey shuddup, no I never. (*To* **Kathy**.) Tell 'er, Mum.

Kathy Don't wind im up, Becs, go n' brush yer teeth.

Mike Yeah, go n' brush yer yellow teeth.

Rebecca You love my yellow teeth!

Rebecca *does a big smile right in* **Mike**'*s face, as there's the honking of a car horn outside.*

Brian Oh Christ, there he is. Herbie Goes Bananas bang on time.

Kathy *grabs* **Mike** *and* **Rebecca**'*s cereal bowls from his hands, as* **Brian** *sneaks a half-bottle of whiskey into his inside suit pocket.*

Mike 'Ey, gi'over . . . –

Kathy Both o'yer brush yer teeth, yer've got a bus to catch.

Mike Not for fifteen minutes, the 97's not due for fifteen minutes.

Kathy Alright, well walk round the back o'the Toll Gate and get the 48, it won't kill yer.

Mike Can't I finish me Sugar Puffs even?

Kathy Well, yer dad managed 'is breakfast on time.

Mike Yeah, because I were desperate for the bog and he's in there for about an hour. And he dunt 'ave to leave half hour early t'drag my bloody sister up Roe Lane like a pillock.

Kathy Yeah, and as soon as he gets the company car it'll be his turn to drive her there like a pillock. In the meantime, try actin' a bit more mature . . .

Mike I am mature!

Brian You've 'ad enough Sugar Puffs.

Rebecca (*to* **Brian**) I've got pig-tails today, look.

Geoff *enters, poking his head in.*

Geoff Mornin' all mornin' all – you about ready, Bri? I'm parked on double-yellows as it is.

Brian Alright, Pac-Man, let me finish me drink.

Geoff *exits.*

Rebecca (*calls*) I've got pig-tails today, Uncle Geoff!

Kathy No one's sayin' yer not mature, we're sayin' you do as yer dad n' me tell yer, we're the grown-ups round 'ere n' **we just so happen to know . . . –**

Kathy (32) **– it doesn't make any sense at all.** There's nothin' on these instructions about pressin' them together. Which one's play and which one's record?

Mike (12) It says so on the buttons, Mum, use yer eyes.

Kathy Which one's record, sorry?

1982

Saturday May 9th (Early Evening)

Mike (12) *is eating crisps as* **Rebecca (8)** *uses scrunchies to tie his hair into bunches, while . . .*

Brian (32) *and* **Kathy (31)** *are crouched in front of the new Betamax video player, with an instruction booklet.*

Brian (32) God knows, um . . . –

Brian *presses eject – the tape ejects – and* **Brian** *and* **Kathy** *laugh.*

Kathy Yer've ejected it again!

They push the tape back in.

Brian Wait wait wait, it's the button there. The one with the big red dot –

Kathy You're a big red dot.

Mike At the same time. Yer press play n' record at the same time. D'yer want me to do it?

Brian/Kathy No.

Mike Are we still goin' Video City after?

Brian 'Ere, try pushin' 'em both together, look.

Mike Should go down Video City in Firth Park. Hanif says they've got *Zombie Lake*, *Zombie Flesh Eaters*, *Zombie Holocaust* –

Brian We're rentin' *Fox and the Hound* and that's the end of it –

Mike Arr, what? She's already seen it about ten times.

Kathy Rewind first.

Brian What?

Kathy Press rewind first.

Rebecca (8) You be Copper, I'll be Todd.

Mike I don't want to be Copper, you be Copper – gi'oer / messin' with my hair a minute.

Brian Rewind what? We haven't taped anythin' yet. Christ, I'm surprised anyone makes it out alive in that hospital o'yours.

Kathy Maybe ask yer new best mate Mrs Thatcher to work it out.

Brian She's got enough on 'er plate with the Falklands. – Look, so you press play n'I'll press record. One, two, three . . . –

Kathy One two three now?

Mike (*to* **Rebecca**) Stop messin' with my hair I said.

Brian / After three press play n' record together. **One, two, three and . . . –**

Mike (12) **– he's goin' to start shaggin'** 'er now, look. Yer can properly see him goin' in n'out 'er fanny.

Hanif (12) Massive jugs though 'ant she?

1982

<u>**Wednesday September 7th (Evening)**</u>

Mike (12) *and* **Hanif (13)** – *both in pyjamas – watching a German porno on the video. There's a bottle of Merrydown cider.*

Mike (13) 'Ant she though I know! The mechanic bloke covers 'em in Castrol GTX in a minute. Starts stickin' 'is thing between 'em like.

Hanif (13) Mad.

Mike It is mad, yeah – I thought yer'd seen this before.

Hanif Yeah course.

Mike Me dad's got loads of 'em hidden in the attic, 'e'd die if he knew. – 'Ere, watch now, look! Watch what she does, look!

They watch.

Mike/Hanif Oh naow! / I told yer dint I?

Rebecca (*off*) Mike, gi'oer now!

Hanif That's funny sort of.

Rebecca (*off*) It's half past ten, Mum said!

Mike You watch, he's goin' to spunk on 'er face any minute.

Rebecca (*off*) Yer know yer'll get us both / in trouble if yer don't –

Mike *pushes the portable gas heater in front of the living room door.*

Mike (*as he does so*) 'Ave you got an 'ard on yet?

Hanif Yeah, course.

Mike I'm already well 'ard me, look. Do you pull yer foreskin back?

Hanif No, it were snipped like.

Mike Same, yeah. Wayne Clay says he uses a wet flannel.

Hanif Wayne Clay is a wet flannel.

Mike Yer know Phillip Lockwood had it off with Karen Hargreaves at Glossop Road Baths?

Hanif Karen Hargreaves is a slut.

Mike I know, she's exactly like Kim Wilde or somert, yer can see right up 'er skirt durin' Physics, *and* she were the first bird in our year to grow pubes. I bet I'm goin' to have it off with 'er next.

Hanif No yer never –

Mike Yes I am 'never'. Phillip Lockwood's a slaphead. Phillip Lockwood dunt even have a video.

Hanif So? I don't 'ave a video neither.

Mike Yeah 'cause you live in Kelvin Flats n'yer don't even have yer own bedroom.

Rebecca (*off*) Mike, I mean it, now –

Hanif Shuddup, yes I do, and yer should see Faisal's house. They've got a microwave, a ZX Spectrum n' about three different tellies.

Mike Gi'oer, don't lie–

Hanif Yeah, me n' Irfan Zebb went up Southey Green to watch *Thriller* at theirs last Easter. We played Manic Miner n' Jet Pac.

Rebecca (*off*) Mike, come on –

Mike Why weren't I there?

Hanif Eh?

Mike Why were Irfan Zebb round Faisal's n'not me? Yer know I wanted to watch *Thriller*, I've been practisin' me moonwalk, remember?

Hanif Well, yer don't know Irfan, do yer?

Mike Yeah, we were in *Bugsy Malone* together n' Faisal's in our Form Group. 'Ow come yer hangin' out wi'them without tellin' me?

Hanif Can't we watch *Rocky Three* or somert? I thought you had *Rocky Three*.

Mike Gi'oer *Rocky Three*, *Rocky Two*'s the best n' we're meant t'be gettin' into this now aren't we?

Hanif *Rocky Three*'s got Mr T.

Mike N' Mr T's rubbish when 'e's not in the *A Team.* (*Shoves his hand down the front of his pyjamas.*) 'Ere, come on Hanif, I bet I can spunk before you, look.

Hanif Piss off, no –

Mike Promise I won't tell anyone or owt. Think about Karen Hargreaves.

Hanif I don't care about Karen Hargreaves, put on *Enter the Dragon* or somert.

Mike (12) Shuddup *Enter the Dragon*, this is practice int it? I bet yer me n'Karen are goin' to be boyfriend n' girlfriend by time I turn thirteen. You'll still be hangin' out with **Faisal n'I'll be –**

Phillip (13) . . . **punch him, Karen,** go on! Slap 'im round the face like I did!

Mike (13) (*struggles*) Alright, gi'oer –

Karen *slaps* **Mike**.

Mike Gi'oer will yer? I 'ant done owt!

Phillip Now kick 'im in 'is tiny pubeless balls.

1983

Thursday June 9th (Day)

Mike'*s 13th birthday.*

All in school uniforms, **Phillip Lockwood (13)** *holds* **Mike**'*s hands behind his back, egging* **Karen (13)** *to hit him.* **Nicole (13)** *and* **Hanif (13)** *are watching on.*

Mike (13) *is struggling to break free.*

Karen (13) Get lost, I'm not touchin' 'is balls.

Phillip (13) Boot 'im, go on.

Mike (13) Please, I'm sorry, . . .

Phillip Fat fuckin' cry-baby, look.

Nicole (13) Arr, gi'oer Phillip, it's his birthday –

Phillip I know it's 'is birthday, you invited us didn't yer, Mike? That's what yer Paki-mate said anyway. 'E invited us over, dint 'e, Hanif?

Hanif Yeah, no, definitely . . . –

Phillip Talkin' shit behind my back, callin' me a slaphead. Some fat fuckin' blubber-mountain nobody likes, even curry-boy hates yer. Tellin' everyone 'e was goin' to have it off with Karen.

Karen Arrr naow, 'e never said that! / Like I'd ever 'ave it off with 'im!	**Nicole** (*laughs*) Oh my god, shame!

Phillip Hanif said 'e saw 'im wankin' over yer that time. (*To* **Mike**.) You had yer knob out dint yer, fatty? Big fat hard on for Karen like Jabba the Hutt. 'Ow about yer get an 'ard on for us?

Mike Please, Phillip, me dad'll be home soon . . . –

Phillip Shut yer face, take yer clothes off.

Mike No –

Phillip Get yer knob out n'give us all a laugh.

Karen I feel sick, can't we go Wimpy?

Phillip 'Ere, grab 'im, Nicole. Pull 'is pants down, Hanif.

Hanif What now, like?

Phillip Pull 'is pants down or I'll tell Irfan n' Faisal that you sucked 'im off down Mosque.

Mike No, wait –

Hanif *joins* **Phillip** *grabbing* **Mike**, *pulling his clothes off.*

Mike Hanif, wait! Me dad –

Phillip No one cares about yer arsehole dad. **Yer dad's –**

Geoff (36) **– too good for yer own good** sometimes. We're in a monetarized economy, yer can't go around prioritisin' everyone else's problems. This is 1983 –

Brian (34) It's not a question of priorities, it's about not throwin' our employees under the bus. Yer not goin' to make me do that to 'im, Geoff, it int right.

1983

Monday 3rd October (Evening)

Post-work, **Geoff (36)** *joins* **Brian (34)** *at home. They drink and smoke.*

Geoff Yeah and yer know if it were up to me –

Brian How's it not up to you? It's your bloody business –

Geoff (36) Regional manager, Bri, there's a difference. – Look, I know how fond you are of 'im, Bri, we all are –

Brian (34) It's not about bein' fond, it's the fact he's fifty fuckin' seven and he'll never work again if we let 'im go now. How'd you like to be his age on the dole?

Geoff He's a good worker, he'll find somethin' else. Few more year he'll get 'is pension.

Brian If he's such a good worker, why yer tellin' me I 'ave to go n' give 'im 'is cards tomorrow mornin'?

Geoff Because we're squeezed enough as it is. We're competin' with China now.

Brian Yer know he's worked on that yard since he were nineteen years old?

Geoff I've worked there since I were nineteen year old and I don't want to end up like 'im, do you? Yer still want yer pay rise n'yer company car?

Brian Christ, well all I can say is yer lucky Kathy's not 'ere. Yer know **I'm already –**

Brian (35) – **lookin' at the owner of a** brand new Vauxhall Astra outside.

Mike (14) (*as he enters*) I know, Mum said.

Brian Yer can see out the window, look. Bright green hatchback, smells beautiful on the inside. B Reg.

Mike (*sitting with his tea*) Yeah.

1984

Friday June 29th (5.45 pm)

Mike (14), *in his school uniform, enters with a plate of chops, chips and peas. He sits on the sofa with it. He has a black eye or is bruised – clearly been fighting.*

Cartoons on TV.

Brian (35) Yer Uncle Geoff's only got an X Reg. 123 miles per hour with yer foot down. –

Kathy (34) *enters, with two plates of chops/chips for her and* **Brian**. *She passes* **Brian** *his plate and sits with her own.*

Brian (*cont.*) Go for a quick spin after tea.

Kathy (34) Well I don't know if yer want to be goin' 123 miles per hour down Burngreave Road.

Brian All yer rastas down Catherine Street do.

Kathy Be my guest if yer want t'get arrested.

Brian 'Ave to get it onto the Autobahn this summer then, eh? No speed limit at all there. Ferry over to Rotterdam – drive through France and into Germany. Hire a caravan –

Kathy Fantastic, yeah.

Brian Beats Blackpool Illuminations in the pourin' rain though dunt it?

Kathy Beats the Droitwich Free Festival at least.

They eat. Pause.

Brian Mike . . .

Mike (14) Yeah, no –

Brian Quick trundle down Video City won't hurt. Rent out *Ghostbusters* or somert.

Mike *Ghostbusters* int out yet.

Brian Well I don't know, whatever yer want. One o'yer horror films. Zombies in the supermarket.

Kathy He's into 'is social realism now. Ken Loach, Mike Leigh –

Brian Well we all need a laugh, don't we?

They eat.

Pause.

Brian *The Wicker Man*, now that's a good film. Britt Eckland –

Kathy I dunno, Bri, he's got that homework?

Brian Which homework?

Kathy Get 'is grades on track, stop 'im truantin' every other day. Last thing he needs is another report card now he's picked 'is options.

Brian Options, yeah. We all need options in life.

Kathy The essay he's been workin' on. *Of Mice and Men*.

Brian Steinbeck, good. What d'yer think of Steinbeck, Mike?

Mike Mm, 'e's okay, I dunno.

Brian I could tell yer one –

Rebecca (10) *enters, in her primary school uniform, clutching her foam E.T. toy, and a plate of chops/chips. She sits on the floor, near* **Mike**.

Brian (*cont.*) – or two things about Steinbeck, I read 'im meself at O level. Course *Grapes of Wrath* or not, it's not everyday yer the owner of a brand new Vauxhall Astra.

Mike Maybe, yeah.

Brian Want t'tell them bastards that. – (*Sees* **Rebecca**.) Oop, sorry, pardon my French. (*To* **Mike**.) Want to do somethin' about that black eye at least. Scrappin' again?

Kathy I've spoken to 'is form tutor, it's fine. Better 'e's supervised than disappearin' into Derbyshire where no one can find 'im. Wanderin' round Dronfield on his own.

Brian Hope they came off worse at least –

Kathy Told 'im the best thing 'e can do is ignore them. (*To* **Mike**.) You just ignore them from now on don't yer, Mike? (*To* **Brian**.) They'll know about it in four years when they're on the dole and 'e's startin' 'is degree.

Mike Yeah –

Kathy Exactly.

Mike No, yeah, just what yer said, dad. Video City n'that.

Rebecca *holds up her E.T. toy in front of* **Mike**.

Mike Take the car out after tea.

Brian Alright then, yeah –

Rebecca (*as she does so*) E.T. phone home, E.T. phoooone hoooome.

Kathy Okay, Becca, don't –

Rebecca When I'm sad I think about nuclear war.

Kathy You do what? /

Brian Who said anyone's sad? No-one's sad are they, Mike?

Mike (*to* **Kathy**) Can I take this up to me room now, please?

Kathy Fine yeah, if yer must.

Rebecca (*gets up*) Love you.

Kathy/ **Brian** Love you. / Love you, Becca, don't be gettin' sad now.

Rebecca *and* **Mike** *take their plates and exit.*

Brian *and* **Kathy** *eat their dinners, the telly on.*

The BBC news report about Orgreave – the police battering and arresting miners.

Long pause, as they eat.

Kathy *gives* **Brian** *a 'look'.*

Brian I'm suckin' on the bone, I always suck on the bone.

Long pause.

Kathy 'Ad two more suicide attempts on the ward. Blokes like that. Miners. Blokes your age.

Brian Well, yer don't 'ave to worry about me . . . –

Kathy I didn't say I was worried about you, why would I be worried about you?

They eat.

It's this lot – the bloody police batterin' ten types of shit out of the strikers. Someone should beat the o' crap out o' them don't yer think?

Pause.

I said someone should –

Sudden loud music playing from upstairs – Duran Duran "Rio".

Oh crap, not Simon Le Bon again. (*Calls up.*) 'Ere, Becca! Becca love, **yer need to turn it down, there's –**

Sudden loud music from the new hi-fi/CD system in the living room – "Easy Lover" by Phil Collins and Philip Bailey.

Kathy (35) **– . . . kids next door,** you'll wake them.

Brian (36) No no, wait for it to kick in, wait! Wait for it, and . . . –

The chorus kicks in –

1985

Friday 7th June (Evening)

Brian (36) *shows off his new hi-fi system to* **Kathy**.

Brian *sings along to "Easy Lover", dancing around* **Kathy**.

Kathy (35) Tragic, Brian, really –

Brian I mean, yer'd never get that on vinyl. The quality, Kath, yer can hear everythin'. – 'Ere –

Brian *grabs a CD of Kate Bush's "Hounds of Love" off the top of the hi-fi.*

Brian (*as he does so*) Feel it, go on. Dolby Digital, no scratches. Yer can even spread jam on it if yer want.

Kathy Oh yeah, I bet yer'd love to spread jam on Kate Bush.

Brian I'm serious, Kath, it were on Tomorrow's World. Stamp on it, spit on it, stick it in the Breville. I mean, **it's all –**

Brian **– . . . for a good cause, Sean.**

Sean (37) All for a good cause? You think Status Quo give two shits about a bunch of starving Ethiopians they've never met.

Kathy Well, we gave money and we've never been anywhere near Africa.

Brian Good for us.

Sean Right, good for you, you won't see me giving a penny.

1985

<u>Saturday 13th July (Afternoon)</u>

Live Aid and Status Quo are performing "Rockin' All Over the World" on the telly.

Brian, **Sean (37)** *and* **Jules**, *are watching the concert, drinking beer and one of those '80s cartons of wine with the fancy plastic tap.*

Kathy Oh come on, Sean, David Bowie'll be on soon. Freddie Mercury –

Jules (*imitating Bob Geldof*) Just give us yer fuckin' money, Sean!

Sean You're telling me Ethiopia doesn't have the money to feed its people? That it couldn't find the money elsewhere?

One – you're buying into the colonial perspective that all Africans are weak and uncivilised and that they'll always need white people before they can help themselves, two – this whole thing is just one big Thatcherite plot to distract us from the real issues . . . –

Kathy Thatcherite plot! I'd hardly accuse Bob Geldof –

Sean Bob Geldof's an egotistical prick who hasn't sold a decent record in ten years.

Jules Midge Ure.

Sean Yeah, well I'm sure Midge Ure's accountant's not complaining – the royalties for that Band Aid shite. – Where's the concert for the poor starving kids in this country, right, Kath?

Brian (*to* **Kathy**) Where's Mike, is 'e out today?

Kathy In 'is room I think.

Brian Wankin' 'is cock off like Adrian Mole. 'Ere, 'ave a cheesy puff.

Brian *sits on the edge of the sofa, sharing the bowl of cheesy puffs with* **Kathy**.

Kathy Well, no of course –

Jules Ignore him, he's / doing it on purpose.

Sean What about the six million unemployed right now, do you think they know it's Christmas? Where were Queen or U2 when the miners were on strike? Where were Paul Young or Nick Kershaw?

Kathy Red Wedge.

Sean My arsehole Red Wedge.

Jules I don't know, making a living? Where were you, Sean, were you on the picket?

Sean Which picket?

Jules Well, you brought it up. How many miners do you actually know, Sean?

Sean Oh, come on –

Jules Compared to the starvin' kids on the news, it's not a trick question. How many miners, how many redundant fucking steelworkers, . . .? –

Sean Well, Kathy's dad –

Jules Not includin' Kathy's dad or Yosser Hughes.

Brian Yosser Hughes.

Jules Characters on the telly don't count.

Sean Yosser Hughes wasn't a miner, for fucksake.

Jules Alright, so how many strikers, how many coal miners do you know?

Sean Well, of course not me personally –

Jules Course not you personally, I don't know any miners or fucking steelworkers either. Neither does he, neither does she, they're a tiny minority –

Kathy Oh right, so Orgreave never happened?

Jules No, I'm askin' him what's the difference between them n' those emaciated kids on the news he's never met either?

Sean Nothing, I'm talkin' about this fuckin' charade.

Jules Sat there goin' about Thatcherism like we all live on some cobbled street fuckin' Hovis advert out the 1930s when yer've actually done pretty bloody well out of her.

Brian It's true.

Kathy What do you mean 'true'? /	**Sean** Alright, sure, whatever / you say, Jules.

Kathy *snatches the bowl of cheesy puffs off* **Brian**, *and makes to leave.*

Jules / Yer'd rather we were back in 70s under Callaghan, would yer? You bought shares in British Gas for Christ's sake, Sean, / come on –

Kathy "Then they came for the Jews and I did not speak out because I was not a Jew."

Jules Oh, gi'oer, Kath, don't you start – /

Brian Kathy . . . –

Kathy "Then they came for me and there was / no left to speak out for me."

Brian / Alright, well done, let's all try to . . . /

Jules Yeah, and yer missin' the point –

Kathy Oh, I'm missin' the point? I can't believe what I'm hearin' from you of all people, Jules.

Jules Okay, don't throw a tantrum – /

Sean (*to* **Brian**) Want a wee bit more wine in that glass?

Kathy Tantrum?! Yer want to spend a day at my work, see how ordinary people have it there –

Jules Hey, I'd be / happy to come down – /

Brian We are ordinary people, that's the point.

Kathy Not like this we're bloody not. – Yeah alright, Jules, come n' see what I have to put up with 365 days a year – bring yer mortgage n' yer gas shares too. Yer know if it were up to me I'd trade the lot to have Freddie Mercury or Bob Geldof or **any one of them so-called –**

Kathy (36) **– vegetarian meals yer** mentioned, so yer'll have to make do with toad in the hole.

Rebecca (12) I'll have to do what, sorry? No shuddup –

Rebecca *removes her Walkman headphones.*

Rebecca – I said about the frozen nut bakes, dint I?

Kathy No, well they didn't have any.

1986

Friday April 25th (Late Afternoon)

Rebecca (12) *is on the sofa, listening to her Sony Walkman.*

Kathy *holds* **Rebecca**'*s dinner on a tray.*

Rebecca No yeah they do.

Kathy Well, yer dad n' I went all the way round, n' neither of us couldn't see them –

Rebecca (12) At Asda, yer've got to go to Asda.

Kathy At Asda, yeah, in the frozen section. Some frozen bloody nut bakes I had to ask the lad at the counter for n'that he'd never heard of, pair of us stood there like headless chickens. – No offence . . . –

Rebecca None taken.

Kathy Look, yer must've had this a thousand times, Rebecca. You love toad in the hole n' Smash –

Rebecca That's like askin' me to eat a human baby.

Kathy It's a sausage.

Rebecca Try tellin' that to its mother.

Kathy Alright, so yer'd better go hungry then 'adn't yer?

Rebecca Thanks.

Kathy Okay?

Rebecca Okay, yeah, thanks. So I'll just starve to death then, shall I?

Kathy Well, that's your choice.

Rebecca Yeah, and these poor animals don't 'ave any choice at all, do they?

Kathy That's because they don't 'ave the intelligence.

Rebecca Alright, so why not eat Mike and Hanif?

Kathy Rebecca . . . –

Rebecca If it's all about intelligence – why not eat gay people with AIDS who dint wear a condom?

Kathy 'Ey, now mind your language –

Rebecca What about all the Russians who decided to live next door to Chernobyl power plant before it exploded – shall we bung them in the oven too?

Kathy No . . . –

Rebecca No, because we're all goin' to die anyway aren't we, Mum? We're goin' to be stood on the Moor lookin' up at some mushroom cloud like in Threads.

Kathy Alright, well there's no point cryin' about it, Rebecca –

Rebecca Am I cryin'?

Kathy No-one's actually droppin' any nuclear bombs any time soon –

Rebecca How do you know, are you the Kremlin?

Kathy Well, because I'm a lot older than you . . . –

Rebecca So old yer can't even face facts when they're starin' you in the face.

Kathy Alright, so I'll nuke you a baked potato, there's no meat in a baked potato.

Rebecca They bash 'em on their heads n'they try to get away.

Kathy Who, the potatoes?

Rebecca No, the pigs, Mum, it int funny. They bash them on their heads with shovels –

Kathy I know it's not funny, I know.

Rebecca So what yer tryin' to turn me into a murderer for?

Kathy Yer've got women's problems.

Rebecca What?

Kathy No, maybe I mean – 'ave yer, love? Hormones, women's problems?

Rebecca Oh my god, shame.

Kathy Alright, so I'll just leave it here in case yer change yer mind.

Rebecca Why would I change my mind? You never change your mind. You still think we should all be listenin' to the stupid Beach Boys when Madonna's sold miles more records than them.

Kathy Yer know that if we didn't eat pigs they'd stop breedin' 'em altogether?

Rebecca They don't need us to help 'em breed.

Kathy Yes they do –

Rebecca Since when 'ave you ever helped a pig have it off?

Kathy Well, I'm not talkin' about me personally. When yer look at agriculture –

Rebecca That dunt make any sense, Mum, even

Kathy Look, yer know full friggin' well it makes sense, Rebecca, I'm talkin' about agriculture, just stop **makin' life so bloody –**

1987

Monday August 24th (Early Afternoon)

The television is on – Neighbours in the background.

Mike (16) *is sitting on the sofa, holding a can of beer and, importantly, a sheet of paper with his O level grades printed on them.*

Brian *and* **Kathy** *– with wine are looking at his results.*

Kathy (37) **– difficult to get those** kind of results, Mike, that's brilliant. –

Brian (38) Clever little sod int 'e? / Don't know who he takes after.

Kathy That's even better than yer did in yer mocks. B in History –

Brian One B, four Cs –

Mike (16) D in German.

Brian D in German, aye – who gives a scheisse.

Kathy Well, a D int bad considerin' they 'ad 'im down for a U last year. More than enough for yer t'start yer A levels now.

Brian Get away from those dickheads at Firth Park at least.

Kathy Fresh start up at Parkwood College, then yer'll be off to university before we know it – thank you, a Labour government.

Brian Thank you, Harold Macmillan.

Kathy (*kisses* **Mike** *on the cheek*) London or Edinburgh or somewhere decent. Oxford or Cambridge.

Brian (*nudges* **Mike**) Ooh Cambridge, fancy lad. (*To* **Kathy**.) I thought you hated public schools.

Kathy (*as she exits*) It's called social mobility.

Kathy *exits the living room, into the hallway*

Brian Yeah, well as long as yer don't mind bein' surrounded by posho bum-boys.

Brian *peers at the slip of paper – with* **Mike**'*s O level results – on it.*

Brian You alright?

Mike (16) Yeah yeah –

Kathy (*off*) David Frost went to Cambridge. Alan Bennett, Jonathan Miller.

Brian "Yeah yeah" – how yer feelin'?

Mike Yeah, um –

Rebecca (13) – *dressed like Madonna with black lace gloves and top etc – enters with an armful of ring binders full of artwork and pencil case.*

Mike (*cont.*) – relived I think, thanks.

Rebecca (*sitting on the floor*) I got As in every subject on my last school report.

Brian Yeah alright, Rebecca, everyone knows yer god's gift. (*To* **Mike**.) See that Phillip what's-'is-face while yer were down there?

Mike No, um –

Brian *punches* **Mike** *on the arm and exits, moving into the hallway.*

Brian (*as he goes*) 'Im n'that Hanif dickhead probably lookin' forward to a career on the bins – (*To* **Kathy**, *off.*) 'Ere, Magnus Magnusson, shall we open that champagne?

Kathy (*off*) Can't yer wait a bit maybe?

Brian (*off*) Dom Perignon though.

Kathy (*off*) So? It's not much past lunchtime, I'll be on the floor by the time we get to the Candytown tonight.

Brian (*off*) / That's precisely the idea, come on.

Kathy (*off*) No, you come on –

Brian (*off, laughs*) No, you come on –

Kathy (*off, laughs*) I'm stayin' sober, Bri, end of. It's not every day yer find out **yer son's got a –**

Mike (16) *peers at his grade sheet, then . . .*

He shows it to **Rebecca**, *who inspects it.*

Pause.

Rebecca Four Cs and a B? That's rubbish.

Mike Try tellin' them that.

He screws the sheet up and chucks it (playfully) at **Rebecca**'s *head.*

As **Rebecca** *arranges the art from her ring binders,* **Mike** *necks the last of his can of lager, as –*

Mike, **Kay** *and* **College Friends** *are singing/shouting "Heaven is a Place on Earth" by Belinda Carlisle, starting from the fifth word of the chorus, then so on, until . . .*

1988

Friday November 18th (Night)

. . . he is joined by his very drunk **College Friends**

Mike (18) *opens the living room door and pushes the* **College Friends** *out of the room.*

(including **Kay (18)***), singing/ shouting.*

They are all holding pint glasses or bottles. **Kay** *holds a half-eaten kebab.*

He shuts the living room door, keeping **Kay** *trapped in the room.*

Still singing, **Mike (18)** *drunkenly lifts* **Kay** *up (or attempts to).*

Kay (18) Oh my god, put me down!

Mike – *singing – twirls* **Kay** *around.*

Kay For fucksake, Mike, I'm goin' to drop me kebab –

Mike *collapses on top of* **Kay** *on the sofa, and starts laughing.*

Kay Gi'oer, yer not even funny, yer know?

Mike *starts kissing* **Kay***'s face and neck.*

Kay Alright stop. Stop it, Mike, dint I tell yer back in Stonehouse not to mix tequila with Strongbow? Yer goin' t'feel like shit and we've got Social Stratification first thing. Miss Beadle wants us to lead the group discussion on class mobility.

Mike (18) Fuck class mobility, give us yer kebab.

Kay You've already had a kebab.

Mike Give us yer kebab, I'm . . . –

Mike *grabs* **Kay***'s kebab.*

Mike – . . . takin' it to another level. 'Ere –

Mike *scrambles up and over to the CD player, rapidly putting on a CD of Gregory Abbott's "Shake You Down".*

Mike – don't you move, Karen, alright? Don't you move from that chair . . . –

Kay Who the hell's Karen? I'm Kay, remember? Kay, yer drunken slob –

"Shake You Down" comes on loud – and **Mike** *turns to* **Kay**, *moving and dancing.*

Mike 'Ear that? Yes! Another level though, right? Let me do it-do it-do it to yer, Kay –

Kay Oh my god, you're tragic.

Mike *takes a fat (erotic) bite from the kebab, and moves closer to* **Kay** *– dancing, singing along to the song.*

Kay Yer do know my ex is just upstairs? (*Calls.*) 'Ere, Huss! Huss, get down 'ere a minute!

Kay *makes to leave, but* **Mike** *blocks her way – still dancing.*

Kay Alright, now yer just bein' bang out of order . . .

Mike What's wrong? Turnin' you on? So sexy, I swear –

Kay Yeah, except yer've never actually slept with anyone ever.

Mike Shake yer down good I will. (*Grabs* **Kay***'s waist.*) Shake yer down, grease you up –

Kay Shut up, 'grease me up'. Where's yer parents, Mike?

Mike You stay 'ere with me. Me n' you, we're goin' to have babies. Big beautiful babies.

Kay Except that's never goin' to happen 'cause we'll be in completely different cities next year.

Mike So? We're breakin' the mould.

Kay No, I'm stayin' in Sheffield n' you're goin' to Thames Polytechnic, remember? Chances are we'll never see each other again once exams are over. I'm just goin' to end up back at SADACCA, aren't I? Finger-paintin' with the kiddies or fillin' in housin' forms – you're like . . . dead fuckin' smart when yer put yer mind to it, Mike, yer can do a lot better than me.

Mike *lets go of* **Kay**.

He moves to the CD player and turns it off.

Mike Dead smart.

Kay Yeah, yer'll probably meet someone much more –

Mike Yer don't like me, do yer?

Beat.

It's alright, I get it. If there's one thing I'm not, it's dead smart.

Kay Oh come on, don't be –

Mike Hit me if yer want.

Kay What?

Mike Hit me, go on. Slap me across the face.

Kay (*laughs*) Alright, don't be stupid – (*Calls.*) 'Ere Huss, get down 'ere a minute!

Mike What yer laughin' at?

Slaps himself round the face.

Hit me fuckin' 'ell, will yer?!

Kay *dashes out of the room, . . . –*

Mike Yeah, go on, piss off like yer always do.

. . . and **Mike** *slams the door shut. He staggers across the room, over to the telephone.*

He dials a number. The sound of music – The Pixies "Monkey Gone to Heaven" – and voices upstairs becomes louder.

Mike *picks up the remains of the kebab, and eats as the phone is answered . . .*

Mike (*on the phone*) Hanif?! Hanif, it's Mike! Mike from school, yer pillock, where are yer?! . . .

What? . . . So where is 'e then, tell 'im I'm callin'. . . . Tell 'im it's Mike, 'e knows who it is. He fuckin' knows who it is . . .

He drops the phone, makes for the door.

Don't know anythin', do I? Don't know fuckin' . . .

He trips and collapses.

Mike (*on the ground, passing out*) – . . . anythin' anymore, Kay. Dead smart, Thames Polytechnic – yeah, you'll fuckin' see. Fuckin' show all o'you when I get back. **When the fuckin' –**

1989

Saturday November 11th (Morning)

Kathy (39) *is hoovering,* **Brian (40)** *is dozing on the sofa.*

TV is on the BBC News report on the fall/ demolition of the Berlin Wall.

Kathy (39) – **Berlin Wall's come down**, look.

But he's drifted off to sleep again.

Kathy *runs the hoover over* **Brian**.

He stirs.

Brian (40) Eh, what?

Kathy (39) Berlin Wall, look. They're pullin' it down.

Brian (40) Oh, right. That's good.

Kathy *hoovers for a few more moments, then . . .*

Switches the hoover off. Carries it out, exits.

Brian *watches the news, until . . .*

He seems he has a pain/itch, and he slides his hand down the front of his jeans.

He feels around his testicles, when . . .

Kathy *re-enters, and he quickly pulls out his hand.*

Kathy (*as she enters*) Looks like Mike finally got round to it.

Brian Hm?

Kathy Mike. I said it –

She holds a birthday card in an envelope that's just been posted, and – as she speaks – she opens it.

– looks like he finally got round to sendin' you a card. Are you alright?

Brian Yeah yeah, fine. Knackered.

Kathy Well, if yer'd ask Geoff for a day from time to time. Be nice to see you when yer not fast asleep. 'Ere –

She places the card on the table. It has a big '40' on the front.

Hardly Steinbeck, but it's the thought that counts. More than we can say for yer daughter.

D'yer think yer should speak to 'er?

Pause.

Brian –

Brian Now they can enjoy McDonald's like the rest of us.

Brian *gestures to the TV.*

Brian East Berlin. Now they can enjoy Coca-Cola n' McDonald's like the rest of the monetised –

The Stone Roses' "One Love" – suddenly blasts from a bedroom upstairs.

Kathy *winces and moves to the living room door –*

Kathy (*calls up*) Rebecca please, not this one again! How can you revise with that racket?

The music is accompanied by the noise **Rebecca (15)** *and her friends laughter/chatter* (*off*).

Kathy (*calls out*) Becca love, it's ten o'clock in the mornin'! 'Ey come on now, **there's –**

Kathy (40) **– . . . someone – Nigel or Nathan** I think – at the door for yer.

Rebecca (16) Which Nigel? There's two Nigels.

1990

<u>Friday 28th September (Early Evening)</u>

"One Love" continues from the pirate radio station, Hardcore FM, on the portable radio.

Kathy I don't know, dreadlocks n' a woolly jumper, he says he's parked on Abbeyfield Road.

Rebecca (*to* **Janey C**) Spiral Nigel wicked, I told yer, dint I? – oh ye of little faith – 'ere, grab us me Vicks vape. –

Rebecca (16), **Davey-Boy**, **Melissa** *and* **Janey C (all 16)** *are blatantly sharing a spliff, getting psyched-up/ready for a night out.*

Melissa *rolling a spliff, wearing headphones,* **Davey-Boy** *is already off his face, throwing shapes and gurning.*

Rebecca *moves to and whips the headphones off* **Melissa**, *with –*

Rebecca (16) – Melissa, move yer batty man, it's time! You n'all Davey-boy.

Davey-Boy (16) (*throwing shapes, gurning, to* **Kathy**) Smooth like margarine on yer tongue!

Rebecca 'Ey –

As she speaks, **Rebecca** *pulls on her psychedelic hoodie, ties her dreadlocks back.*

Rebecca (*back to* **Kathy**) – did he say owt about where the convoy's goin' to be later?

Janey C (16) I can't see it nowhere.

Rebecca Where we just sat, knobhead. Look – the Vicks and me phonecards, – (*To* **Melissa**.) you grab that radio in case, sexy. – (*To* **Kathy**.) 'Ey, don't tell me he just knocked n' buggered off or did yer just leave 'im on the step n'not say owt?

Kathy No, well, I weren't payin' attention –

Rebecca 'Cause if he thinks we've already gone then the whole night's fucked n' we might as well go into town and no one wants to go into town on a Friday.

Kathy Stop talking for two minutes.

Rebecca Arrr, look at you – come on, come 'ere.

Melissa (16) Man, can't we just go to Kiki's or Occasions or somert? I'm sick of drivin' up n' down the M1 all night.

Rebecca *gives* **Kathy** *a hug.*

Rebecca (*as she does so*) Someone needs a big squishy hug I reckon.

Davey-Boy *joins* **Rebecca**, *hugging* **Kathy**.

Davey-Boy I fuckin' love you, Rebecca's mum.

Kathy Yep, I love you too.

Rebecca 'Ave yer got a spare phonecard on yer?

Kathy Phonecard?

Melissa Let's go Cairo's, it's house night.

Rebecca Shuddup Melissa. (*To* **Kathy**.) Go get yer purse, I bet yer've got one in yer purse.

Janey C Don't need phonecards, we've got Hardcore FM. DJ Face n'Goosey –

Rebecca Yeah, well the last time we waited on DJ Face n' Goosey we ended up playin' shithead at Woodall Services all night, that's why they invented phonecards, yer blob. – (*Passes spliff to* **Kathy**.) 'Ere, yer can . . .

Rebecca *ushers* **Kathy** *out of the living room.*

Rebecca . . . take this up to Dad while yer lookin'. Nice bit o'rocky from Donkeymans, mellow buzz.

Rebecca *shuts the living room door, blocking* **Kathy** *out.*

Rebecca (*to* **Janey**) Where's the doves, yer twat?

Janey C Which doves, yer twat?

Melissa (*shows bag of pills in her pocket*) Here's yer fuckin' doves, d'yer want to frisk me for them?

Rebecca / Arr wicked. You legend, Melissa –

Rebecca *kisses* **Melissa** *on the cheek, takes the bag of pills. As she speaks, she hands them out.*

Rebecca – enough so I don't have to think. Spiral's goin' to drive us down CJ's n'then we'll wait for Hanif to bring us the tamazi's for the comedown later. Hanif's safe, man, I've fuckin' known 'im since I were a kid n'e knows like everyone. Knowles Brothers, Blades Business Crew, all yer top dealers up Crookes n'everythin' – **he's like proper –**

Rebecca (17) – **Synchronicity** though, init.

Hanif Synchronicity, yeah.

Rebecca Me n' you together, Hanif. Like Celestine Prophecy n'that. Like Jonathan Livingstone Seagull.

Hanif Yer makin' me cock go soft.

1991

Monday January 21st (Night)

Rebecca (17) *and* **Hanif (21)**

are dry humping on the sofa.

Seal's "Deep Water" is playing on the CD/tape deck.

Rebecca (17) Can yer see my aura?

Pause.

Rebecca Hanif . . .

Hanif (21) Yeah, course –

Rebecca What colour is it?

Hanif I dunno, blue?

Rebecca Green blue more like. I reckon your aura's blue like Aquarius.

Hanif Taurus.

Rebecca Gi'oer, you're no way a fuckin' Taurus. Mani from Stone Roses is a Taurus. So's Janet Jackson but she can fuck off 'cause she's only famous 'cause of Michael, and he's a Virgo like me. You're more like Apache Indian or somert.

Beat.

Rebecca Hanif –

Hanif Yeah, no –

Rebecca Saddam Hussein's a Taurus. Would you join the Army if they made yer? Would you like go n' kill innocent babies in Iraq? I reckon Mike would, I bet he'd be the first in Desert Storm.

Hanif No, Palestine.

Rebecca Where?

Hanif Fuckin' Israeli's, init – just shuddup a minute –

Rebecca What d'yer mean, shuddup? We're only dry-humpin'. Yer allowed to talk when yer dry-humpin' – 'Ey, gi'over . . .

Hanif – *kissing* **Rebecca** – *is trying to pull her underwear off.*

Rebecca – don't do that. Hanif man, don't, I'm on my period.

Hanif That were last week.

Rebecca What?

Hanif Yer said that last week. At Occasions, remember? On the bean bags in the chill-out room.

Yer said it were time o'the month –

Rebecca I was off my head, I'll say any old shit. And it were the Palais, not Occasions, get yer facts straight.

Hanif Well, it dint sound like any old shit. Yer know it's alright if yer nervous –

Rebecca Who said I'm nervous? – 'Ey, fuck off, it int *Crystal Maze* –

She pulls **Hanif***'s hand away from her underwear.*

Rebecca – I'm tryin' to engage with you, aren't I?

Hanif Engage wi'me in yer bedroom then.

Rebecca Yeah, n'I've told yer a million times, my wall's right next to my mum's. She'll only get jealous if she hears us goin' at it like dogs. – 'Ere, shift over that way a second, yer erection's diggin' into me.

Hanif It's meant to be diggin' into yer.

Rebecca Can't we just have sex with our eyes?

Hanif Oh for fucksake, man –

Rebecca I've told yer, it really flippin' hurts when yer do that –

Hanif Be better off havin' a wank. Fuckin' Anthea Turner or somert.

Rebecca Gi'over, Anthea Turner. If yer goin' to have a wank over anyone it should be Carol Smillie or Wendy James.

Hanif (*stops dry-humping*) Alright then, sorted.

Rebecca I mean, there's no shame in it, is there? You n' Mike used to get yer willies out all the time when we were kids.

Hanif Nice one, yeah –

Hanif *pulls himself free.*

Hanif . . . are yer goin' to pay me for that whizz?

Rebecca Eh? What yer / stoppin' for?

Hanif / The fifteen pound you owe me for trips n' the half gram o'whizz. The pink champagne I give you on tic the other night – am I some sort o'charity case?

Rebecca Yeah, I know, yer'll get it when me child benefit comes through.

Hanif Don't make me go back to the Knowles brothers n'tell 'em you aren't payin' up. Swear to god, Becca, don't take me for a pussy.

Rebecca I'm not though, I love you.

Hanif (*laughs*) What?

Rebecca I love you, Hanif, always have.

Hanif *grabs his trainers, puts them on.*

Rebecca I feel safe with you, I mean. We look good together, don't we?

Hanif Yeah, so yer can show me off to yer dickhead mates up Norton College? Sell you ganja inbetween exams?

Rebecca We don't do exams, it's a Media Studies BTEC. Yer know if yer'd ever even listen –

Hanif I'm done listenin'. Dry-humpin' like some no-dick bumberclart, I want my dollars.

Rebecca Yeah, alright 'Goodfellas', I'm tryin' to talk to you about important, spiritual stuff –

Hanif What, lightin' a few jossticks n' crappin' on about who killed Laura Palmer? Swear to god, if you think I'm goin' to get my knees broke because of you –

Rebecca Child Benefit, retard, use yer ears. Bloody Seal man goin' on.

Rebecca *marches to the CD player, turns the Seal CD off.*

Rebecca Don't even rate Seal – why dint yer bring that Ned's Atomic Dustbin that I like?

Hanif Yeah, we all know what you like, Becca. Minge-eater.

Rebecca *lobs the CD at his head.*

Hanif I swear to god, don't test me, star –

Rebecca Yeah, or what? Yer goin' to sit there n' cry about it, star?

Hanif *grabs the CD and quickly exits.*

Rebecca Yer'll cry when I call the cops on you n' them faggot bastard Knowles brothers. When they lock you up, yer fuckin' –

Rebecca *follows* **Hanif** *into the hallway, exiting.*

Rebecca (*as she exits*) – lowlife lyin' piece o' shit. Mike's down in London, what are you doin' with yer life? Yer goin' to brag about how yer got yer sad little end away finally? Well, go on. Tell 'em whatever yer want about me, tell 'em I'm the best sex you've ever had if that's all it meant to yer! I mean, it's not like **any of 'em ever gave a –**

1991

Tuesday 31st December (Afternoon)

Brian *is in his dressing gown.* **Kathy** *is feeling/inspecting his testicles.*

Rebecca (17) (*enters*) – **shit about New Years**, but some of us do have actual / friends to –

Kathy (41) / In a minute, Becca, I told yer!

Rebecca Oh my god, no – What's 'e got 'is bits out for?

Brian (42) Alright, it's not what it looks like, Becs.

Rebecca No, that is disgusting –

Kathy Tie yer robe up, Brian, go on.

Rebecca Why is everyone so fuckin' disgustin'! Oh my god, **you're like –**

1992

Wednesday 1st January (2.00 am)

Rebecca (17) *grabs the small living room bin – containing a newspaper and empty cans of lager – and pukes into it.*

A party can be heard from her bedroom, with her friends singing/dancing along to Vic Reeves and The Wonder Stuff's "Dizzy".

Rebecca – **uuuuUUUUU-URRRRRRR!!**

She pukes into the bin again.

Rebecca – uuuuUUUUU-URRRRRRR! Jesus Christ.

Kathy *enters, in her night-dress/dressing gown, holding a pint glass of water.*

Kathy (*as she enters*) Might want t'get this down yer, Becca.

Rebecca (17) – uuuuUUUUUURRRRRRR! Ohhh . . .

Kathy *moves and sits next to* **Rebecca***.*

Kathy Come on now, get yerself / together –

Rebecca – uuuuUUUUUURRRRRRR!! Oh fuck. Oh fuckin' 'ell.

Rebecca *violently pukes again, clutching onto* **Kathy***'s night-dress.*

Kathy Well, yer'd be better off doin' that in the bathroom don't yer think?

Rebecca Yeah, n' Dad's in there with the fuckin' door locked again! What's he doin' in there anyway?

Kathy Alright, I'll ask, I'm sure he won't be long.

Rebecca Sat on the bog doin' 'is fuckin' crossword for hours. Yer won't though will yer, Mum?

Yer never ask 'im to do anythin' 'e dunt want, yer just let 'im fuckin' – uuuUUURRRRR!

Kathy *pats her on the back.*

Rebecca Oh my god, I'm dyin'.

Kathy Well, yer not.

Rebecca Oh god –

Kathy Believe me, I know death when I see it, you're not even close.

Rebecca I hate my life.

Kathy Look, yer'll be alright once yer drink some water. And yer certainly not the first person to drink too much on New Year's Eve. Sounds like some of yer friends might be goin' the same way.

Rebecca Will yer tell 'em to go? Will yer tell 'em to go home now, please?

Kathy *grabs some tissue from her pocket and hands it* **Rebecca**, *who starts to cry.*

Rebecca Please, Mum? Please –

Kathy Well, I'm not sure they'll listen to me. You invited 'em, you have to deal with it, I think.

Rebecca I'm sorry.

Kathy They're your friends, I can't be responsible for / them n'all.

Rebecca I'm sorry I fucked up.

Kathy What?

Rebecca No, that I'm such a fuck up for yer.

Beat.

Rebecca Yer know if I'd been more like Mike . . . –

Kathy Oh give oer, yer nothin' like yer brother.

Rebecca I know I'm not, that's problem. If I'd been more like you even.

Kathy Oh . . . –

Rebecca Happy just to plod along. The way you just get on wi'it, Mum, yer know? I love that.

Like yer don't let anythin' get to yer, yer not even bothered –

Kathy Not bothered, right.

Rebecca Same borin' job all yer life. Happy just to come home n' watch telly every night.

Don't do anythin', don't go anywhere –

Kathy Okay, thanks –

Rebecca I'd love that, I think. No, I would, I'd / love that . . . –

Kathy / You ever helped save someone's life? You ever watched someone fade out – deteriorate until their wettin' the bed n' cryin' out for whichever god that int even there? When there's only you n'them n'you 'ave to find the right words to say.

Rebecca Um, no –

Kathy You ever pushed a funnel up at old man's arse?

Rebecca (*laughs*) Um, no –

Kathy Try changin' the sheets on twenty piss-stained beds with some –

Melissa (17), *in her New Year's party outfit, enters.*

She carries a large glass of water and moves and sits next to **Rebecca**.

Kathy (*cont.*) – stoney-faced Sister watchin' over yer. Then yer'll see what's –

Melissa (17) (*as she enters, to* **Kathy**) Sorry, d'yer mind?

Kathy Oh . . . –

Melissa Sorry, I thought I'd best stay down 'ere with 'er a bit. 'Ere, Becs . . .

Rebecca *grabs* **Melissa**'*s hand.*

Melissa Worried yer might've ditched me again.

Rebecca No.

Melissa Still up f'watchin' *True Romance* with me later?

Rebecca Yeah.

Melissa Patricia Arquette.

Rebecca Yes please, yeah.

Melissa *takes a bobble and ties back* **Rebecca**'*s hair.*

Melissa Get yer hair out yer pretty face at least. (*To* **Kathy**.) That alright?

Kathy No no, you go ahead, that's –

Kathy *edges to the living room door.*

Kathy – fine, Melissa love, you, um . . . **keep 'er hydrated, n' I'll –**

1992

Thursday August 27th (Midday)

Kathy (42) *escorts* **Brian (43)** *back from hospital. He holds a crutch with one arm, walking with difficulty.*

Kathy (42) **– 'ang onto me arm, come on. My arm,**

Bri, yer don't want to fall on yer arse.

Brian (43) It's not me arse I'm worried about.

Kathy Steady I said, go get on the armchair, I've put the soft cushions down f'yer, look.

Brian (43) Fuckin' 'ell fire, –

Brian *slumps into the armchair, dropping his crutch.*

Is this 'ow Adolf Hitler felt down below? No wonder he invaded Poland.

Kathy (42) That's 'cause 'e dint 'ave scrotal supports. Rest n' yer'll forget all about it. Splash of Dunhill?

Brian *nods, and* **Kathy** *takes and sprays the Dunhill aftershave on* **Brian**'*s neck.*

Kathy Your lucky day. They're doin' three for two at the W.H. Smith's on Fargate, look.

Kathy *places two books on the coffee table in arm's reach of* **Brian**.

Kathy *Diana: Her True Story* and *The English Patient.* Keep yer quiet, won't it?

Brian *English Patient*, eh? Did they chop off his bollock n' all?

Kathy Well, they've got prosthetics now, Bri.

Brian (*laughs*) Eh?

Kathy Course we can think about all that later. At the hospital, I mean. Prosthetics.

Brian Alright, fuckin' 'ell, one thing at a time.

Kathy Sorry, no, it's just the doctor mentioned –

Brian Yeah, I know what 'e said, thanks.

Kathy Once yer've recovered, I mean. Sorry, I just thought . . . –

Pause.

Sorry, I know, just ignore me.

Brian Are we alright?

Kathy What?

Brian Are we alright?

Pause.

I need us to be alright.

Pause.

Kathy . . . –

Kathy I don't know, yeah. / Just shuddup –

Brian I don't know, yeah?

Kathy Shuddup a second, Brian, yer need yer codeine pills.

Brian Codeine, aye, top buzz. –

Kathy *exits.*

Brian (*cont.*) – That n'the morphine, could 'ave a party, couldn't we? Flashback to 1968.

Brian *sings the final line of the chorus of "Feel-Like-I'm-Fixin'-to-Die Rag" by Country Joe and the Fish. When he reaches the final word of the chorus, –*

Lights off – complete darkness, into –

Rebecca (17) **– 'ear us down 'ere anyway.**

Melissa (18) Yer sure? What about yer mum?

Rebecca Flat about by eleven o'clock usually, long as we don't make any sudden noises.

Melissa What if I want t'make some sudden noises?

1992

<u>Friday August 28th (Late at Night)</u>

In the darkness, the sound of muffled movement.

Sound of kissing.

Melissa (18) What if I can't 'elp meself, eh?

Sound of kissing.

Rebecca (17) Well then, I'll just 'ave to smother yer then, won't I?

Melissa Ooh, smother me, Rebecca.

Rebecca Smother yer between me legs, yer mean. Entry forbidden, no survivors –

Lamp turns on, revealing **Brian (43)** *(covered in a makeshift sheet) sitting on the armchair, and half-dressed* **Melissa** *and* **Rebecca** *on top of each other.*

Brian (43) – 'Ow's that for a sudden noise?

Rebecca *and* **Melissa** *scream.*

Brian Oh, don't mind me . . . –

Melissa *grabs her clothes and darts out of the room.*

Brian . . . I'm doped up on Fentanyl anyway.

Rebecca Alright, I'm sorry, I didn't know . . . –

Brian What?

Rebecca Sorry for everythin', Dad, yer . . .–

Rebecca *grabs her clothes, makes to leave.*

Rebecca . . . really shouldn't 'ave 'eard that. Yer know it's not what yer think –

Brian Who the hell cares what I think.

Rebecca No, it was for college, it was a project for college, a role-play for a video were makin' –

Brian Nice arse.

Rebecca What?

Brian Yer girlfriend. Nice arse, well done.

Rebecca Oh . . .–

Brian Rather her than a stream of knobhead boyfriends f'the next god knows how long. And I hope she knows how bloody lucky she is n'all, yer can tell 'er I said that – 'ere –

Brian *switches the lamp off.*

Better go n'find 'er before she sprints off down Rutland Road. Enough nutters around as it is. I mean, **yer've got to –**

1992

Saturday October 3rd (Evening)

A party for **Mike***'s graduation.*

Brian *and* **Kathy**, **Sean (44)** *and* **Jules (44)**, *and* **Mike (22)** *with his girlfriend* **Nina (23)**. **Mike** *and* **Nina** *wear graduation gowns.*

Sean *noodles on his guitar. There's lots of drinking and smoking.*

Kathy **– celebrate 'is graduation properly, even if it did mean drivin' up n'down the M1 in a single day.** Should've seen it, Jules. Down by the Thames, everyone in their posh gowns –

Jules (44) Congrats, Mike.

Mike (22) Thanks.

Jules Yer know I remember when 'e were just that high.

Brian 'E's still that high.

Kathy Gives us a chance to meet 'is new girlfriend finally. Top up, Nina?

Sean (44) Oh sure, you can count me in. How a 'bout a round of strip poker while we're at it? – Sorry, Mike, but Christ she's stunning, isn't she?

Nina (23) Cover your ears, Mike.

Sean Ooh-hooh. And wears the trousers by the sound of it.

Nina Well, I try my best.

Mike Got a first in Psychology.

Sean Okay –

Nina Psychology with a minor in Black British Literature.

Sean Black British Literature, that does sound minor. Took you all of what, five minutes?

Nina Well, it's not riddled with antisemitism like George Bernard Shaw and Yeats.

Sean (*to* **Mike**) I like her, she's funny.

Mike Yeah –

Jules (44) He's doing my head in, Kath.

Kathy (44) He'll be fine, I'll get the Trivial Pursuit out soon. 'Ere –

She passes the card to **Jules**.

Kathy – see what Becca n' 'er girlfriend wrote 'im.

Jules *reads the card, as* **Kathy** *continues pouring drinks for* **Nina** *and* **Mike**.

Kathy They're down at the Leadmill seein' Pulp.

Jules (*reading card*) What's Pulp who?

Kathy I don't know, some local band with a stupid name.

Jules (*passes card back*) Someone to look after yer though, int it?

Kathy Hm?

Jules When yer get old, I mean. Good yer've got two good kids, they're good.

Kathy Oh, / yeah most of the time.

Jules / Sorry, I'm drunk. Ignore me –

Brian Play a tune, Sean, for fucksake.

Brian *hands* **Sean** *his guitar, as . . .*

Mike (*to* **Nina**) Don't worry, he's just showin' off.

Nina I'm not worried, / it's funny.

Mike No, I mean we don't have to stay if we don't want.

Nina It's funny seeing you in your own space. Your natural habitat.

Mike Eh?

Nina *kisses* **Mike**.

Nina You're allowed to put your arm around me, you know.

Mike I've got the portable telly upstairs. Watch *Red Dwarf* or somethin'.

Nina I don't want t'watch *Red Dwarf*, stop being so paranoid. I'm fine, honestly, –

Brian Top up Nina? Mike?

Nina Yes please, thank you, Brian –

Brian *tops up* **Mike** *and* **Nina***'s wine glasses.*

Mike Thanks, Dad yeah, that's plenty.

Kathy Shut up, that's what we're here for isn't it? (*To* **Brian**.) Grab us that bottle of ouzo, Bri.

Jules Waste o' good oxygen.

Sean (44) Who's a waste of oxygen, sorry?

Jules You are, Sean.

Sean Well, after twenty-five years, there's bound to be a few old wounds.

Jules Fifteen of those years on the dole.

Sean So what? You're hardly saving the world stamping overdue books at the public library.

Jules I happen to like it there.

Sean And I happen to like being on the dole. I get up when I like, I don't have to answer to anyone –

Jules And all at the taxpayer's expense.

Sean Christ, it's becoming like Maastricht, you can't say anything anymore can you, Nina, eh?

Kathy We were talkin' about their graduation.

Sean Well, let's not. Let's talk about the single currency and the end of British democracy – thank you John Major who has no lips. (*To* **Nina**.) Let's talk about the poll tax or Maastricht. – I know, how about Bosnia and the break-up of Soviet Union.

Nina (23) The I.R.A.

Sean Arr, I like what you did there. A little blow to the chest.

Jules Yer'll get more than a blow in a minute. (*To* **Nina**.) He's been like this for decades, he's never changed –

Sean I choose not to change. I may go grey, but I never change. (*To* **Nina**.) Sorry, where's your accent . . . ?

Nina North London.

Sean Okay, yah 'North London' –

Brian Behave, Sean.

Mike We're moving into her parents' place. Kentish Town.

Sean Moving in already? (*To* **Brian**.) He takes after you.

Nina My dad runs an education consultancy. I'm joining the diversity tteam. Addressing the systemic bias in schools and further education.

Kathy Oh really? That does sound fancy.

Nina Mike's coming aboard too, aren't you? Field coordination. Liaising with schools, streamlining logistics, –

Kathy (*to* **Mike**) Really, are you? Yer never said. /

Brian Good for you, Mike, well done.

Nina Making sure data flows smoothly from classroom to consultancy.

Kathy And your dad doesn't mind? He knows he's only just graduated.

Mike Mum –

Nina No, well it's entry-level, but it's perfect for / someone like Mike.

Mike Full time, decent wage.

Kathy How come yer never said?

Mike That's why we're here, Mum. That's why we decided to come up tonight. How come Rebecca's not here?

Nina It is a key role –

Jules (*to* **Kathy**) University, see?

Nina Very dynamic.

Brian Dynamic aye, that's our Mike all over. /

Sean Sounds like a complete head-fuck.

Nina Honestly, we're lucky. Most of our uni mates are going straight on the dole or stacking shelves.

Jules We just plod along, don't we, Kath?

Kathy Eh, sorry? Plod?

Sean Well, stacking shelves or not, she's probably the most beautiful girl I've ever met, Michael, and, I've been around a good / few fucking years.

Brian (*to* **Nina**) / It's alright, he's been using the same line since the mid-sixties.

Jules Earlier than that, Brian, I think. The fucking potato famine.

Nina Oh no, I don't mind, I can take a compliment.

Brian It's how he got out of National Service.

Jules It's what he first said to me at any rate. "The most beautiful girl this side of Sheaf Market."

Brian Hey, that's my chat-up line!

Some laughter.

Sean (*laughs*) Alright, so I'm a sad pathetic plagiarising old cunt, what can I tell you?

Jules Well, some honesty at last –

Sean And I'll admit I did also – for my sins – attempt the same line on your wife some years ago now, Brian, yer big one-bollock bastard. But in my defence –

Mike / He did what? /

Kathy Ignore him, he's pissed.

Brian Yer didn't / stand a chance.

Jules He's pathetic. /

Nina Fleetwood Mac eat your heart out.

Sean / – stand a chance, – No, you're right, I've been waiting on you to keel over for years, you fucking know-it-all eunuch. Working class Tory –

Brian Alright, watch your gob –

Sean (*laughs*) My gob, sure! This gob was my bread and butter once upon a time. – (*To* **Kathy**.) Christ, I fucking hate getting old, don't you?

Sean *starts playing the guitar – "Where Do You Go To My Lovely" by Peter Sarstedt.*

Starting at the second stanza of the first verse, **Sean** *directs his singing at* **Kathy**.

He continues into the chorus.

As he almost ends the first chorus –

Brian *snatches the guitar off* **Sean**.

Sean Sure, I'm a cunt.

Brian *makes to hit* **Sean** *with the guitar*

Jules Alright Brian, don't . . . – / . **Mike** Fucksake, Dad! /
Nina (*laughs*) Oh my god.

Sean I said I'm a cunt, didn't I, Bri?!

The doorbell rings.

Kathy Pizza's here! Go n' –

Kathy *takes the guitar from* **Brian**.

Kathy – fetch the pizzas, Brian, go on. (*To* **Nina**.) The hell are you laughin' at? (*To* **Sean**.) Jesus wept, Sean –

Mike She'll laugh at what she wants.

Kathy Eh? / Oh shuddup Mike –

Mike Don't speak to 'er like that, Mum, / say sorry.

Kathy / I didn't speak to 'er like anythin' – say sorry?! It's 'im what should say sorry. Say sorry in my own house, **are you fuckin' . . . –**

Kathy **– twenty-two-year-old, Mike.**

Pause.

Mike.

Brian Mike . . . –

Mike Yeah, she said. Twenty-two –

1992

<u>Saturday October 3rd (2.00 am)</u>

Mike *eats cold pizza from the box, sipping on a lager can.*

Kathy *sits next to him.* **Brian** *is on his feet, drinking from a bottle of brandy.*

Brian Twenty-two-year-old, think about it.

Kathy You haven't even lived yet.

Mike Define livin'.

Mike *waits for a response, doesn't get one.*

Mike Yeah, see that's what I / thought. Fuckin' clueless –

Brian / Yer've only just graduated, yer've got so many choices still. /

Kathy Alright, there's no need to swear.

Mike And that's what this is, Dad. A choice, an opportunity –

Brian What, some bullshit made-up job? Tyin' yerself down with some girl yer've only just met.

(*To* **Kathy**.) Fuckin' 'ell, he'll be marryin' 'er next.

Mike Maybe I will, Dad, yeah. Maybe I've already picked the ring. How old were you when you first met Mum?

Kathy That were different, things were different back then –

Mike Yeah, and I / happen to love her and she loves me.

Brian / Things were different, yeah –

Kathy Oh grow up, 'she loves me'.

Brian – yer mum only realised she were pregnant before it were too late.

Kathy *looks at* **Brian** *– 'What the fuck?' – and exits.*

Brian Look, why don't yer come 'ome forra bit first, eh? Come back t'yer old room forra few week.

Mike Why, so yer can push me away again?

Brian No-one's pushin' you away, we're family. Please, Mike, after all I've been through these last eighteen months –

Mike I don't care what you've been through.

Brian Oh, come on –

Mike I don't care anymore, I don't. It wasn't even my idea to –

Nina (*enters*) Are you coming to bed now, peachy? –

Nina, *in her nightclothes, appears in the living room doorway.*

Nina (*cont.*) – You know it's almost half past two. (*To* **Brian**.) Sorry –

Brian No no, don't, um . . . – Hi, peachy, um . . . / Nina.

Nina – / I've left your toothbrush on the sink for you. The travel one.

Mike *gets up and exits.*

Nina And you should probably drink a pint of water, too. (*To* **Brian**.) Don't want him hungover for the train back to St

Pancras tomorrow morning. (*Calls to* **Mike**.) Everything okay?

Mike (*off*) Fine, yeah.

Nina (*to* **Brian**) Sorry about that, I'm a terrible micro-manager –

Brian Fine no, same.

Nina Product of Jewish parents and a Montessori education, I'm afraid. I don't suppose you'd be able to give us a lift to the station? In the morning, I mean, with the buses the way they are. It's **just you can't –**

Geoff (45) **– expect me to double-run the accounts** on top of everythin' else.

Brian Alright fuckin' hell, I'm coming, just / let me get my clothes on –

Kathy *enters from the living room, with* **Brian**'s *briefcase and his work clothes.*

Geoff / Every mornin' last week and the week before that. Worse than when we were kids –

1992

Monday December 7th (Midday)

Geoff (45) *is by the living room doorway, holding his car keys.*

Brian (43) Well, I didn't have a choice, Geoff, alright?!

Kathy (42) *helps* **Brian** *get changed.*

Brian (*to* **Kathy**) / Fuckin' hell, you 'eard this? –

Geoff Didn't have a choice, aye, sick leave every other month. Yer know yer should tell that GP of yours how many contracts we've lost to South America if 'e's that bothered about yer head? How d'yer think it looks to our clients when they see yer've left painkillers all over yer desk?

Kathy They're not painkillers, they're testosterone replacement.

Geoff Boo fuckin' hoo, the pound's just crashed, yer'll need more than testosterone when they lay us all off in six month's time. When the government finally –

Geoff'*s mobile phone rings – a brick Motorola MicroTAC. He answers –*

Geoff (*cont., into phone*) Yeah? . . . What d'you mean stuck at Tilbury? It was cleared Tuesday – No,

I don't give a –

He exits into the hallway.

Geoff (*cont., into phone*) – toss what Customs say, it needs to be on site by Monday. (*Beat.*) Alright, tell Clive I'll send 'im a fruit basket.

The front door is slammed shut, offstage – and . . .

Brian *and* **Kathy** *burst out laughing.*

Kathy (*laughing*) Oh my god –

Brian (*laughing*) "The pound's just crashed!"

Kathy (*laughing*) "The pound's just crashed!"

Brian (*laughing*) Fuckin' 'ell, his face . . . –

Kathy (*laughing*) My god, his face though . . . Pop!

Their laughing dies down.

Pause.

Kathy Yeah, well I'd better get / goin' meself, Bri.

Brian Yeah, I shouldn't keep 'im waitin' then.

Kathy *hands the briefcase to* **Brian**, *who makes to exit.*

Brian (*as she exits*) Wouldn't want to feel the wrath.

Kathy No. No, **I guess yer –**

Kathy (43) **– wouldn't want to be** left short, 'ere.

Rebecca (19) (*eyes on the TV*) What?

Kathy 'Ere, look –

Kathy *hands her the envelope.*

Kathy A few more travellers' cheques for yer. Ten more minutes before they close thankfully.

Rebecca Oh . . . –

Kathy Yer dad's idea. Don't let 'im know I agreed.

Rebecca (*peering into the envelope*) Thanks.

Kathy Better than 'avin' a million different currencies rattling around yer purse.

Rebecca Thanks.

1993

<u>Saturday February 13th (Afternoon)</u>

Rebecca (19) *is sitting on the sofa, wearing her long coat and boots, watching the TV. Her hair is dyed a bright colour, and she has a nose ring.*

There is a large packed rucksack, with tent attached, resting on the side of the sofa.

On the TV, it's a BBC news report about the abduction and killing of 2-year-old Jamie Bulger.

Kathy (43) *holds a post office envelope full of travellers' cheques.*

Kathy (43) Yer got everythin'?

Rebecca *nods and turns back to the TV.*

Long pause.

Kathy Wish I could've gone across Europe when I were your age. South of France, Greece –

Rebecca (19) Prague.

Kathy Prague, yeah.

Rebecca Maybe yer should've then.

Kathy What, a single young woman in Czechoslovakia?

Rebecca Czech Republic.

Kathy Czechoslovakia in 1968.

Rebecca *gives* **Kathy** *a 'look'.*

Kathy Suppose yer've got Melissa to protect yer. Just watch when yer crossin' roads won't yer, love? Takes a bit of gettin' used to, everyone drivin' on the right. Make sure yer look both ways before yer cross.

Long pause, they watch the news report.

Rebecca I'm never havin' kids.

Long pause.

Rebecca *turns the TV off.*

Sorry, yeah, I'd better, um –

Kathy Half past one.

Rebecca Half past one.

Rebecca *gets off the sofa, pocketing the envelope, and lifts up the rucksack.*

Kathy Sorry I can't come down to the Interchange with yer.

Rebecca No, Melissa's probably down there already.

Kathy Got yer ticket n'yer passport?

Rebecca *pats her bum-bag.*

Kathy Alright then.

Rebecca Alright, yeah.

Kathy *helps* **Rebecca** *lifting the rucksack on her back.*

Kathy Call when yer get on the ferry if yer can.

Rebecca Yeah –

Kathy Excitin'.

Rebecca Bye then.

Kathy See yer soon.

Rebecca *exits, into the hallway.* **Kathy** *stands by the doorway, watching her go.*

The front door closes, offstage.

Kathy *sits on the arm of the sofa.*

Long pause.

Kathy *gets up and starts tidying up the living room, as –*

MUSIC – MAX RICHTER'S DREAM 13 (MINUS EVEN)

(The music continues throughout the following, until indicated.)

Kathy *keeps tidying up the living room, gathering rubbish and putting it in the bin.*

She takes the filled plastic bag from the bin ***and exits into –***

1994

– with wrapped fish and chips *in a plastic bag.*

Brian (45) *is sitting on the sofa, drinking a beer and watching Have I Got News For You on TV, as –*

Kathy (44) *and* **Brian** *unwrap the fish and chips together.*

Brian *kisses* **Kathy** *on the cheek and gets up, crosses the room* ***and exits, stepping into –***

1995

– Christmas Day, *with a bottle of brandy.*

The TV is on – an episode of Friends.

Mike (25) *and a heavily pregnant* **Nina (26)** *are opening presents of baby toys.*

As **Brian (45)** *enters,* **Mike** *passes him a present.*

Brian *rips open the present. It's an Oasis t-shirt.*

We see (but don't hear) him calling for **Kathy (45)**, *as* **Brian** *pulls the t-shirt over his own shirt.*

Kathy *hears* **Brian** *calling.*

She leaves the fish and chips on the table and ***exits, stepping into –***

– ***the living room,*** *holding an unwrapped of her own.*

She laughs at **Brian** *in the Oasis t-shirt, and passes the present to* **Mike**. *Have I Got News For You remains on the TV.*

Mike *opens the present – a cuddly elephant toy – as* **Kathy (45)** *sits next to* **Nina** *and feels her pregnant belly, feeling for the baby to kick.*

Kathy *motions for* **Brian** *to feel the baby kick, but* **Brian** *says something about needing another glass for the brandy. He crosses the room,* ***stepping into –***

1996

– ***where*** **Sean** (**47**) ***and*** **Jules** (**47**) *are watching the England vs Germany 'Euro 96' game on television.*

Kathy *can be seen (but not heard) calling* **Brian (47)**.

Brian *hands out beer cans and joins them watching the game.*

She leaves **Mike** *and* **Nina** *opening their presents, gets up and crosses the room. She* ***exits, and steps into –***

The game's getting very exciting, and we see (but don't hear) **Brian** *and the others chatting/commenting on the game.*

The TV broadcast Friends remains on stage through the following.

A goal is scored, and they celebrate. We see **Brian** *calling for* **Kathy**, *but he gets no response, so . . .*

1997

– ***the living room,*** *escorting a* **New Labour Canvasser** *from the front door.*

There is a Spice Girls music video on TV.

Kathy (46) *listens as the* **New Labour Canvasser** *gives her New Labour leaflets and a 'Vote New Labour' poster.*

Brian, *taking his can, leaves the others and* ***exits, stepping into*** . . .

– ***the living room,*** *in his work-clothes and briefcase.*

Brian (47) *joins* **Kathy** *talking to the* **New Labour Canvasser**.

Sean *and* **Jules** *continue watching the football game.*

Kathy *takes the New Labour poster and, finding a blob of Blu Tack, starts sticking it up to the living room window.*

Brian *and the* **Canvasser** *are distracted by the Spice Girls on TV.*

Brian *says something lewd about Ginger Spice, making the* **Canvasser** *laugh.* **Kathy** *tells them both to behave, stuffing a bunch of New Labour fliers into* **Brian**'*s hand.*

Brian *laughs, checks his watch. Taking the fliers, he exits, –* ***stepping back into 1996 briefly,*** *to celebrate a goal with* **Sean** *and* **Jules**, *then he* ***turns and exits, into . . .*** –

Kathy *returns to the window, and continues sticking the New Labour poster up, with difficulty.*

The **New Labour Canvasser** *steps in and helps* **Kathy** *sticking the poster up, so . . .*

Kathy *leaves him to it. She takes the Sky remote control and changes the channel to –*

BBC News coverage of the '97 General Election.

Kathy *puts the remote control down,* ***and exits, into –***

Throughout the rest of this section, the New Labour Canvasser continually sticks up then replaces posters on the windows for the next two General Elections – in 2001, then 2005. *And the broadcast of the '97 General Election remains.*

1998

. . . ***Christmas Evening,*** *with a cracker hat on his head, holding a huge box with a brand new Windows PC in in it. (Shreds of wrapping paper still dangling from the box.)*

Brian (48) *puts the PC box down. Catches his breath.*

He takes a sip from his can of lager, then – throughout the following –

Brian *unboxes the PC with some difficulty and dumping the box, polystyrene case and bubble wrap on the living room floor.*

This takes time (until indicated).

Brian *still unboxing the PC.*

Brian *has a coughing fit.*

He grabs tissues from his pocket and spits up blood.

Meanwhile – back in ***1995***, **Mike** *and* **Nina** *unwrap a present that becomes* **Baby Lucas**, *as* ***they slide into . . .***

Xmas 1996, *with* **Nina (27)** *breastfeeding* **Baby Lucas**, *as* **Mike (26)** *tidies away all the wrapping paper.*

He steps into the hall, and returns with a pushchair, wrapped (partly) in wrapping paper, as ***they slide into . . .***

Xmas 1997, *and* **Nina (28)** *places* **Lucas (2)**, *who is crying, into the pushchair.*

Nina *has had enough of the crying and steps out of the room, leaving* **Mike (27)** *to push the pushchair round in circles on the living room floor.*

1999

– ***the living room*** *where the millennium celebrations are on TV.*

Kathy (48) *is talking (we don't hear) on a Nokia mobile – the end of a phone call to* **Brian**.

She sits on the sofa and finishes the call.

She's tearful. Blows her nose with tissues, when –

Fireworks outside! – and . . .

. . . Rebecca (25) *races in, with a bottle of champagne.*

She hugs **Kathy** *and points to the fireworks outside, as –*

He looks at the tissues.

Hesitates, then pockets them.

He returns to the PC, unboxing it.

He's got the PC out of the box, but the box and the polystyrene foam casings are getting under his feet.

He exits, as –

Meanwhile, **Sean** *and* **Jules** *(back in 1995) take their drinks and* ***exit into –***

As **Nina** *re-enters (in 1997), grabbing* **Mike** *by the hand and the* ***exit into –***

– everyone (except **Brian***) –* **Mike (29)**, **Nina (30)**, **Sean (50)** *and* **Jules (50)** *burst into* ***1999*** *room with drinks.*

They hug each other and hold hands and sing (though we don't hear) "Auld Lang Syne".

The **Labour Canvasser** *continues sticking posters up throughout.*

Rebecca *takes her drink and* ***exits into . . .***

Leaving the others singing, hugging, chatting.

This continues for a few moments, until . . .

Mike *and* **Nina** ***exit into . . .*** –

And the millennium scene ***transforms into . . .***

2000

. . . leaving **Kathy (49)**, **Sean (51)** *and* **Jules (51)**, *sitting around nervously, waiting for someone to arrive.*

Big Brother is on TV.

The doorbell (unheard) goes, and **Jules** *exits.*

A moment passes and **Brian (50)** ***enters***, *escorted by* **Jules**.

The unconnected PC (and box etc.) from ***1998*** *can still be seen throughout the following.*

2003

. . . with travel bags, getting ready *to leave for their train.*

Nina (34) *carries a crying* **Baby Alice**.

Teletubbies is on TV.

We see (but don't hear them) bickering about where **Lucas** *is, and what time the taxi is meant to be picking them up, and have they packed everything.*

Mike (33) *double-checks the contents of a travel bag, and* **Nina** *calls for* **Lucas** *from another room.*

2001

. . . the living room, *speaking onto her mobile phone.*

Her eyes glued onto the TV, broadcasting the news of the September 11 terror attack.

Rebecca (27) *continues watching the TV.*

She attempts to roll a cigarette, but it falls apart.

She keeps watching the news.

The scene ***transforms into . . .***

2002

. . . where **Rebecca (28)** *is watching the news report of the US/UK invasion of Iraq.*

She struggles to keep still.

He's on crutches with a bandana over his head. His hair has fallen out from chemo.

Sean *and* **Jules** *watch on, as* **Kathy** *moves over to* **Brian**, *hugging and embracing him.*

Jules ***exits*** (***to make tea***) . . .

Sean *stands and wants to embrace* **Brian** *too, but it's a bit awkward.*

Sean *follows* **Jules** *out,* ***exiting into*** . . ..

Kathy *embraces/kisses* **Brian** *tightly.*

Kathy *tells* **Brian** (*unheard*) *to sit down on the special cushion, then* ***she exits into*** . . . –

Lucas (8) ***enters***, *holding a football, laughing.*

He throws the ball at **Mike**, *who chases him around the room.*

Nina *shouts at them both, trying to calm* **Baby Alice**.

Lucas *pushes* **Mike** *over and* ***exits into*** . . .

2004

. . . **Geoff (57)** ***enters,*** *with a stack of paperwork.*

He sits on the sofa, flicking through a stack of paperwork, ticking things off with a pen.

The X Factor is on TV.

Geoff *takes his mobile phone from his pocket and answers it.*

She texts on her mobile phone.

She attempts to roll a cigarette, but it falls apart.

The doorbell (unheard) goes, and **Rebecca** *exits.*

Pause.

She re-enters ***with*** **Melissa (28),** *who is holding a placard saying "NOT IN MY NAME".*

Melissa *shows* **Rebecca** *the placard.*

Rebecca *takes the placard from* **Melissa**.

She embraces/kisses **Melissa** *tightly.*

. . . (***in 2003***) *leaving* **Nina** (*with crying* **Baby Alice**) *and* **Mike** *to bicker.*

2005

. . . ***and moves straight*** *to the* **New Labour Canvasser** *who is sticking up poster for the 2005 Election.*

Kathy *holds a newspaper, with the headline "BLAIR'S BLUNDER: IRAQ LIES EXPOSED" and has a go (that we don't hear) to the* **Canvasser**.

Kathy (54) *pulls the poster from the window, and shoves it in the* **Canvasser**'*s hand, telling him to leave.*

Meanwhile, **Brian** (***in 2000***), *decides not to sit down and* ***exits into . . .***

Kathy *escorts the* **Canvasser** *out of the room and out of the house.*

We see (but don't hear him) having an earnest work conversation on the phone.

When . . .

Brian (55) ***enters,*** *in work-clothes, carrying a heavy toolbox.*

He dumps the toolbox on the floor.

Geoff – *still talking on the phone – hands* **Brian** *a P45 form.*

Brian *looks at the form.*

He makes to shake **Geoff**'*s hand, but* **Geoff** *quickly gathers his papers and leaves the room.*

Brian *watches him go.*

He screws up the form and ***exits into . . .***

We see (but don't hear) **Nina** *telling* **Mike** *to control their son.*

She leaves the room, exits.

Mike *gets up, makes to follow her out, but stops and thinks.*

He looks at his reflection in the mirror.

Meanwhile, (***in 2002***) **Rebecca** *and* **Melissa** *finish their embrace.*

Melissa *whispers something and exits.*

Rebecca *takes a breath and slides onto the sofa, into –*

2006

. . . *where* **Rebecca (32)** *flicks through a well-thumbed booklet with the cover "THINKING ABOUT ADOPTION?"*

She picks up the litter bin and starts clearing up the clutter.

She turns the TV on: BBC News coverage of the London 7/7 Bombings.

As she clears up the clutter, she finds some tissues stuffed down the side of the sofa.

She looks at the discarded tissues and sees they're covered in blood.

Kathy *fights her tears.*

We see (but don't hear) her calling to **Brian**.

No answer, and ***she exits into***

1998

Kathy (48), ***followed by*** **Brian (49),** ***– both wearing cracker hats, enter.***

Kathy *has a roll of binbags,* **Brian** *has an extension cord.*

Kathy *clears up and tidies up the rubbish,* **Brian** *connects the PC.*

They sit in front of the PC.

Amy Winehouse on the Jools Holland Show is on TV.

Mike *moves from the mirror, and, taking his travel bag, passes through* ***2006.***

He grabs the adoption booklet out of **Rebecca**'*s hand and exits.*

Rebecca *protests, following him out of the room, as the scene* ***transforms into . . .***

2007

. . . late night. *Torrential rain outside.*

The TV is on – a news report on the disappearance of Madeleine McCann.

No one comes in or out.

The storm outside causes the lights and TV screen to flicker, revealing . . .

. . . everything from 1993–2007; the 'Jamie Bulger report' onwards, though the '1997 Election', and up to 'Madeleine McCann report'.

THE MUSIC – MAX RICHTER'S DREAM 13 (MINUS EVEN) – ends/ fades.

Brian *turns on the PC, and –*

Blackout.

Interval.

Act Two

2008

Tuesday 4th November (Late Afternoon)

On the TV, a BBC News 24 report about Barack Obama's presidential election victory.

There is a computer desk fitted into the corner of the living room. **Kathy (58)** *sits at the desk, tapping and scrolling on her mobile phone.*

Brian (59) *is finishing his plate of fish and chips.*

Pause.

Kathy (58) (*of Obama, on the TV*) People thought the same about Kennedy.

Brian (59) People thought the same about Tony Blair. (*Sings.*) "*Things can only get better.*" Remember that? Shittest song ever.

Kathy Well, things did get better.

Brian Yeah, for the Gallagher brothers maybe. Try tellin' that to the shipbuilders in Tyneside or yer grievin' parents in Iraq.

Kathy Things got better, Brian, end of.

Kathy *presses 'send' on her text message.*

She then hits print on the PC – a Sudoku puzzle begins to print out.

Kathy People 'ave very short memories.

Brian Well, yer can't blame 'em, I suppose. No one wants to be reminded of the socio-economic limits of capitalism. Yer think Barack Obama's goin' to be any different to Bush? Watch how he tones down the rhetoric after a few months.

Truth is they've only let a black guy in so they can have a fall guy once the recession kicks in. Chances are they've had it all planned for –

Kathy Sorry, would yer mind shuttin' up now please?

Brian Eh?

Kathy Could yer turn down the cynicism today, Brian, please?

Beat.

Brian Alright, course –

Kathy Thanks.

Brian I'll just, um . . .

Brian *picks up the remote control, attempting to turn the television off.*

Kathy The other remote.

Brian What? Oh . . . –

Kathy That's the Sky remote, yer need the other one. Red button.

Brian *picks up the correct remote control and turns the television off.*

Brian There.

Kathy Thanks, yeah, here's yer Sudoku.

Kathy *hands* **Brian** *the Soduko puzzle.*

Kathy Keep yer quiet, won't it?

Kathy *cleans up his fish and chip wrappers/cutlery, as* **Brian** *takes the pen from his shirt pocket and concentrates on the Soduko puzzle.*

Kathy Need me to do anythin'?

Brian Yeah, yer can book us three weeks in St Lucia if yer want.

Kathy St Lucia – yeah, that's the Italian place just opened on the Wicker?

Brian Above the Space Centre, aye. What time's yer shift this evenin'?

Beat.

Oh fuckin' hell, Kathy –

Kathy Yer'll 'ave to come at me with a chainsaw if yer think I'm going anywhere near that ward.

It's less than a week since the last round of chemo –

Brian Yeah, and there's people in a lot more need than me.

Kathy I'm not leavin' you to mope around here getting dizzy.

Brian I'm fine.

Kathy . . .

Brian Relatively I'm fine.

Kathy Until I find you at the bottom of the stairs again.

Brian That's not going to happen, I've got everythin' I need right 'ere. Coffee, fags, Barack Obama, the old . . . (*Wrestles an iPod from his pocket.*) iPod mini Rebecca got us, look – I mean, who needs CD's anymore, eh? Roy Harper, Pink Floyd, a bit of Arctic Monkeys to keep me down with the kids.

Kathy *gives* **Brian** *a 'look' and exits with the fish and chips plate/wrapper.*

Brian Alright, so I've never been down with the kids, that doesn't mean yer missin' more shifts.

Kathy (*off*) Well, too late 'cause I've already told Rob, so –

Brian Call him back then.

Kathy (*off*) Brian –

Brian Pick up the phone and call him back, I'm still the man of this house.

Kathy (*off*) Yer what?

Brian As the man of the house –

Kathy (*off, laughs*) Yer fuckin' what, yer big lump?

Brian *laughs and becomes light-headed, puts the Sudoku and pen down.*

Kathy *re-enters, holding a tea-towel.*

She sees **Brian** *and sits on the arm of the sofa. She puts her hand on him.*

Pause.

Kathy Bri . . . –

Brian Bog break.

Kathy Yeah?

Brian Bog break, yeah. It's alright, I'll –

Brian *pulls himself to his feet. Using his crutches, he makes to leave.*

– be fine on me own. Fend off the arthritis n'that.

He grabs his pack of cigarettes.

Clear the tubes.

Kathy Oh, Brian . . . –

Brian Better than me creepin' round behind yer back, int it? Don't look at me like that, yer know it's true. Few puffs won't 'urt anyway.

Brian *exits, making his way up the staircase* (*off*).

Pause.

Kathy *returns to the PC, presses buttons.*

Kathy (*calls*) Help me get rid o'this bloody McAfee.

Brian (*off*) What?

Kathy (*calls*) Man of this house, yer can help me uninstall the . . . stupid McAfee thing that keeps slowin' everythin' down, yer can help me with that.

Brian (*off*) Told yer not to install it.

Kathy (*calls*) That's what I'm sayin', yer can help me uninstall it.

Pause – she tap-taps on the keyboard.

Kathy (*calls*) Should get an Apple MacBook, they're a lot faster. More whatsit, more memory.

Brian (*off*) Beatles thought of it first.

Kathy (*calls*) What?

Brian (*off*) Apple. Beatles thought of it first.

Kathy (*calls*) Beatles thought of everything first according to you.

Brian (*off*) That's 'cause they did! An apple, a strawberry, and a girl with kaleidoscope eyes.

Kathy (*calls*) Don't forget the walrus. Oh, that reminds me –

Kathy *pulls her mobile phone from her pocket, opens it.*

Get on Facebook n' see what Michael's up to these days. See if he's put up any more pictures of the grandkids. For all we know, she's probably pregnant again. I mean, it's not like he'd ever get round to **tellin' us even if 'e 'as –**

Kathy (59) *(on the phone)* – **'ad enough turkey** for one day, thanks, there'll be plenty left when yer come round tomorrow . . . Thanks, Rebecca, yeah, you . . . You get back t'yer Jenga n' I'll see yer then, I expect I'll speak to Mike soon enough, yep. Okay, love . . . Okay . . . Okay then, love, you too.

Kathy *ends the call, pockets the phone.*

She takes the television remote and turns the volume up – a carol service.

She sits at the make-shift table and returns to her Christmas dinner, watching TV.

Long pause – as she eats.

2009

<u>Friday December 25th (Daytime)</u>

Heavy snowfall outside.

There's a Christmas tree with a handful of presents under it. A few cards. A decorated, makeshift dinner table has been erected. A turkey dinner (for one) is half-eaten on the table, along with a bottle of gin, a bottle of tonic, and a glass.

An empty chair and a placemat with an empty glass, opposite **Kathy***'s chair.*

Kathy (59), *wearing a Christmas cracker hat, on the phone to* **Rebecca**.

Kathy *pours herself a large gin and necks it.*

She fills up the glass again and goes to drink it, when –

She gets up and moves to the presents under the Christmas tree.

She chooses a small, wrapped present and returns to the table.

She unwraps the present.

Inside is a bottle of **Brian***'s Dunhill aftershave.*

She sprays the aftershave on the back of her hand.

She sniffs it.

Pause.

Kathy *tries to eat again – when . . .*

Her mobile phone rings.

Kathy *picks up the phone, looks at the caller ID.*

She turns the phone off and puts it down.

Pause.

Kathy *takes a swig of gin.*

She presses her face against the back of her hand, smelling the aftershave.

Long pause.

Kathy *takes her phone and presses a button.*

Waits for an answer, then –

Kathy (*on phone*) Sorry, Becca, I was just puttin' the bin out. . . . What's a pocket call, sorry? . . .

No no, that's alright. . . . That's fine, I was just puttin' the rubbish outside anyway.

. . . No no, don't . . . That's fine, **love, I just thought –**

Kathy (60) that's a happy coincidence. I was goin' to call round n' ask if yer might be interested in takin' some of these clothes off my 'ands. For your husband maybe? Few shirts, a couple of jumpers. 'Ere, let me . . . –

Kathy *makes room for* **Safiya (42)** *to come in.*

Kathy – . . . clear some space for you, love, I've got boxes comin' out my arse.

Safiya Sorry, it's just it's nine o'clock now –

2010

<u>Wednesday May 12th (Evening)</u>

There's music playing loudly from the TV –Pixie Lott's "All About Tonight".

Kathy (60), *holding an opened bottle of wine, has just let in* **Safiya**, *the next-door neighbour, who wears a headscarf.*

There are three or four cardboard boxes – one of them has 'BRIAN' written on the side in marker.

Kathy I know it's nine o'clock, I just thought I'd make some room, get organized. Take it to the Oxfam shop if no one else wants it.

Kathy *rummages in one of the boxes.*

Kathy (*as she does so*) You help yerself, Sophie, won't yer? Maybe there's a pair of these jeans yer husband might like.

Safiya Safiya.

Kathy What?

Safiya Safiya.

Kathy Safiya yeah, yer know I see you, um . . . comin' in and out the front or wherever? Out the back in the garden – ugh, through the window I mean, my window. I'm not a stalker or anything, we 'ad an Iraqi family in before you. Then there was Busola, she and her husband were Nigerian.

Safiya Well, it takes all sorts.

Kathy D'yer want a glass of wine? Sorry, let me find you a glass, um . . . –

Kathy *takes a mug that says "BEST DAD" from one of the boxes.*

Kathy Good to finally meet you anyway – there's an Afghan family taken over the off-licence up the road, isn't there? They're really nice, excellent English.

Safiya (*of the wine*) Actually, thanks, I shouldn't –

Kathy Good to see it bein' put to good use. The off-licence, I mean, it's been boarded up for months. I blame Northern Rock. Gordon Brown n' Alistair Darling bailin' out the bastards at the banks –

Safiya Yer know yer telly's quite loud.

Kathy It's what, love, sorry? Loud?

Safiya I mean, it's very nice n'everythin'. My kids bedroom's just through there.

Kathy Oh. Oh, well god . . . –

Safiya And it's a school night, Kathy, they've got school tomorrow. Yer see their bedroom's just through there? Sorry.

Kathy Yeah no, don't you be sorry – Sorry, –

Kathy *turns the TV volume down.*

. . . I can't stand it either, if I'm honest with yer. Whoever this Lady Gaga's meant to be, prancin' around with 'er bottom out.

Kathy *turns on Sky News with the remote – report on the 2010 General Election.*

Be better off watching these two cosyin' up in the rose garden for the tenth time today.

Coalition or not, people have very short memories, yer see? Nick Clegg, the swine. 'E's done nothin' for Sheffield, absolutely nothin'. When yer've lived 'ere as long as I have –

Safiya I know, I'm on the council's environmental taskforce, we've 'ad to deal with 'im sometimes. Typical MP, one eye on the prize. Not a patch on Blunkett.

Kathy Oh right. Right right, so you're environmental . . .? –

Safiya Green City Action, yeah. Yer know if yer ever feel like gettin' involved, Kathy? We've got a few volunteers your age in Burngreave. Nothin' major – gardenin', keepin' the area clean. Park across the road, the heliport. Good folk if yer lookin' to make new friends.

Kathy Oh, I've plenty of friends.

Safiya Okay, great. Great, / sorry, I just thought –

Kathy / No no, I'm quite – quite sociable, Sophie, thanks. There's me work-mates n'my grand-daughter n' 'er two mums. Sheffield's answer to Jane Fonda, jettin' halfway around the world. Muggins 'ere drafted into **babysit while she's –**

Kathy (61) **– off to soddin' Cairo** when there's riots goin' on – are you mad?

Rebecca (37) They're not riots, it's a revolution. The Arab Spring, Mum, read yer *Guardian*.

Kathy What, and so yer goin' to topple President Mubarak now, are yer? You n' the rest of the Muslim Brotherhood prancing down Tahrir Square in yer tights?

Rebecca Someone's got to, haven't they? It's for the kids, Mum, come on. Kids Maya's age – it's important we give them a platform to express themselves.

2011

<u>Tuesday November 22nd</u>

Kathy *is joined by* **Rebecca** *and* **Maya (9)**.

Rebecca *pulls a hold-all bag and* **Maya** *has a stuffed rucksack and a laptop.*

Kathy Oh gi'over "platform", they're on every news channel goin'. I don't see any Egyptians flyin' out over 'ere to march against tuition fees.

Rebecca Why would they march against / tuition fees –

Kathy Exactly, 'cause either way it solves nothin'.

Rebecca What?

Kathy It solves nothin', absolutely nothin'. I mean, I'd understand if yer said you got a kick out of it or if they ever paid yer –

Rebecca They are payin' me, Mum, I'm on an Arts Council grant. I've told yer a million times already, I'm workin' with the Crucible's Creative Learning Department, –

As she speaks, **Melissa (37)** *and* **Maya** *enter, carrying* **Maya**'*s sleepover bags.* **Maya** *has her* Harry Potter and the Half-Blood Prince *book tucked under her arm.*

Rebecca – it's part of their outreach programme. Drama Therapy, Mum, that's my job. – For Christ's sake, we only talked about it the other day, –

Kathy When the other day?

Rebecca At Blue Moon the other day, you 'ad that apple n'cinnamon crumble. – Look, it's only five nights and Maya doesn't mind, she's got 'er laptop n' 'er books.

Kathy (*sits down at the PC, presses keys on the keyboard*) Yeah, in the middle of the school term –

Rebecca / Four days actually, because Melissa's back from 'er yoga retreat on Friday so she can pick 'er up then – it's got nothin' to do with / school, she's got exceptional grades.

Kathy It's not her I'm worried about. Maya, I love lookin' after Maya, that's not the point, it's the fact yer think I'm sat around twiddlin' me thumbs all day. This printer that never works –

Melissa (37) Do yer need a hand wi'that, Kathy?	**Kathy** No, yer fine, Melissa, I'm fine – yer know she never listens, she's never once listened.

Maya / It's fine, I'll go round Cillian's.

Rebecca You will not go round Cillian's, yer can stay with yer grandma like we agreed. – (*To* **Kathy**.) What, I've not what? Stop slammin' / the keys like that.

Kathy / I said I'm not sat around 'ere twiddlin' me fuckin' thumbs all day long, I've got / rosters comin' out of my arse. Patients in need, half the NHS in therapy. Runnin' between wards like a / blue arsed fly.

Rebecca / Switch yer shifts then, I don't know.

Kathy Switch my shifts?

Rebecca Switch yer shifts, Mum, fuckin' 'ell, yer used to do it all the time for Dad. (*To* **Melissa**.) See, didn't I tell yer she'd forget?

Kathy When he couldn't walk or swallow his pills maybe. When he were laid out on the bathroom floor in a puddle of his own puke.

Rebecca Well I wouldn't know would I, Mum? 'Ow would I know that, eh?

Maya (*to* **Kathy**) Time of the month, yer should be nice to her.

Beat.

Maya Time of the month, Gran –

Rebecca (*to* **Maya**) 'Ey, stop bein' so smart all yer life.

Maya No, but I 'eard you on the phone –

Rebecca Never mind what you 'eard, when I were your age, I were still dressin' up as Scooby Doo.

Maya Whatever man, you're the boss. Can I go up n' finish me vlog now?

Rebecca If yer must, I'm sweatin' buckets.

Kathy (*to* **Melissa**) I'm sorry, Melissa, my head's all over the place n'I've been up since six o'clock.

Melissa It's fine, she's got her book and her Samsung.

Kathy If it's not Rob at work, it's EDF energy or Yorkshire Water or our Mike beggin' for another handout. **Yer know yer more than –**

Kathy (61) **– welcome anytime** you want.

Mike (41) Alright, fine –

Kathy Would've switched my shifts if I'd known. If yer'd given me some notice.

2011

<u>Wednesday December 21st (Early Evening)</u>

The room is set for Christmas, presents under the tree.

Mike I said it's fine, Mum, don't stress about it.

Kathy Does Nina know you're here?

Mike *gives* **Kathy** *a look.*

Kathy Alice n' Lucas? Expect they'll want t'know when their dad's comin' home.

Mike (41) – *in a dishevelled suit – is sitting on the armchair, finishing a microwavable lasagne on a tray on his lap. He has a travel bag by his feet.*

Kathy (61) *sits on the chair by the PC, with a cup of tea. Dressed for work.*

Mike I don't know, no. Lucas just turned sixteen, I'm everythin' that's wrong with the world.

Kathy Thought yer might've brought Alice up to visit at least. Christmas in three days.

Mike Christmas yeah, they've got their mum for that.

Mike *finishes his food; cracks open a can of lager.*

Mike No, I . . . I don't know, Mum, just yet.

Kathy Well, I'll let them know yer here in any case. Yer mobile still on incomin' calls only?

Kathy *takes her mobile phone from her pocket.*

She makes to send a text but hesitates.

Anythin' you want me to tell them?

Pause.

Mike.

Pause.

Mike –

Mike Thought I'd get the bus up Firth Park tomorrow I thought? See the old school, the old Brushes building.

Kathy Okay then, right. God, well, they knocked down Brushes a few years back I think, it's a sixth form college now. Big glass front, all very high-tech.

Mike Concorde Park then.

Kathy What?

Mike Have a walk up Concorde or somethin'. Go together, couldn't we? Somethin' to do.

Kathy Well, yes we could.

Mike Fuckin' loved that park. I remember I tried gettin' off with Karen Hargreaves up by the playground. Me n'Hanif. Bottles of Merrydown from the Threshers after school one night. Back in third year.

Kathy Then yer'll need to catch the 75 or 76. FirstBus not Stagecoach. Or yer can get the number 20 and walk from Lane Top.

Mike Thanks, yeah.

Kathy Yer goin' to go n' look for 'er? Karen thingamabob. Maybe she's still up there.

Mike Kay or whoever.

Kathy Who?

Mike Kay from college, yer met 'er once. "What d'yer want to go out with someone like me for? Yer'll find someone dead smart I bet."

Pause.

Nina called me 'retard' this mornin'. That's the word she used. 'Retard.' Two seconds before throwin' the doorkeys at my 'ead.

Kathy Oh –

Mike It's fine, she's got friends she can talk to. High achievin' friends. Holland Park, Muswell Hill.

Kathy So she doesn't know you're here, then?

Mike Jumped the barriers at St Pancras. Hid in the toilet when the inspector came down at Leicester. No barriers at Sheffield, simple.

Kathy *thinks about texting again but then puts her phone away.*

Long pause.

Kathy Look, we've all had it tough from time to time –

Mike Really – have yer? Rebecca doesn't have it tough.

Kathy Rebecca can't function if things aren't tough. Perhaps if you ever picked up the phone n' spoke to her ever.

Mike And 'ave 'er goin' on about Ghanian fuckin' sweat shops ' 'til I'm slittin' me own throat?

Mike *lights a cigarette.*

Pause.

When 'er dad's business went bust I thought I'd wait it out, wait for the phone to ring. That's what they told us anyway. After the crash, "Just ride it out, mate. Any day now, things'll pick up". Turns out I didn't go to public school and so I'm not good enough for the top jobs. Too qualified for the shit jobs and yer've got a queue of fuckin' foreigners eatin' 'em up for four quid an hour anyway – nice one Labour, throwin' the doors wide open. Can't afford owt for the house, I've got zero to contribute to the bills or school trips. Two entitled kids who think it's all about becomin' rich n' famous when I can't even afford twenty pound into their trust fund at the end of the month. My credit ratin's shit, I can't afford the mortgage and, yeah, I'm bein' referred to counsellin' on account that I'm pullin' my own marriage apart. Yer know I was this close to goin' down Brixton n' gettin' stuck in with all the thugs smashin' up JD Sports in the riots last month? Turns out I'm not qualified for that either. Not ghetto enough, too white. Shame really, thought I'd cadge meself some decent trainers at least.

Kathy What's wrong with those trainers?

Mike Nothin', yeah, Alice picked them out. Dad trainers, dad jeans, dad belly.

Mike *picks up* **Brian**'s *urn.*

Mike Bet 'e's pissin' 'imself up in heaven. (*Opens the lid, looks inside.*) Knew it all along dint yer, Dad? "Choices, Mike, opportunities." Some things yer can't help, I guess.

Kathy There's ten pounds in me purse.

Kathy *finds/opens her handbag, removes her purse and takes a tenner out of it.*

Kathy If yer wouldn't mind pickin' up a thing of milk for me?

Mike Yeah.

Mike *takes the tenner,* **Kathy** *takes the urn* (*placing it back on the side*).

Mike Yeah , thanks –

Kathy I'll log on later, transfer a couple of hundred. Should keep yer goin' forra bit?

Mike Okay. Okay, yeah, that's –

Kathy Long as yer need, Mike, yer know that. Help me out round 'ere a bit, can't yer? Round the house or whatever. Whatever yer need, **yer know yer've got –**

Kathy (*to* **Nina**) **– loads of work lined up** with 'is dad's old tools. Jack of all trades now, aren't yer, Mike? Anyone needs their front gate fixin', trouble with their pipes. – (*To them both.*) Now who wants a hot chocolate n'a mince pie?

2012

Thursday January 5th (Early Afternoon)

Nina (43), *has arrived – with a large hold-all.* **Kathy** *has just escorted her inside.*

Mike Yes please, Mum. /

Nina No thank you, Kathy.

Kathy (*to* **Nina**, *as she exits*) Should be back on his feet in no time, you'll see.

Kathy *exits.*

Mike (*to* **Nina**) It's only temporary.

Nina Okay, fine, she just said, –

Mike *makes to kiss* **Nina**, *who pulls away.*

Mike Mum's goin' over to Rebecca's so we've got the big bedroom. Thought we might get a takeout, go / over everythin' –

Nina / Good, yeah, my return train's at three-thirty, so that gives us about half an hour. Yer might want to check through the case, make sure I haven't forgotten anything.

Nina *dumps the bag by* **Mike**'*s feet.*

Nina Not much. Your underwear, a few shirts and jeans. Your Wii console and some of your games.

Mike Oh –

Nina Rest is in storage, so you'll have to pick those up yourself. Okay?

Mike Okay. Okay, yeah.

Nina Okay?

Mike Okay, yeah – yer got any charlie on yer?

Pause.

No, sorry, I just / thought –

Nina Even if I did, Mike.

Mike For old time's sake?

Nina And my solicitor should be in touch about taking your name off the mortgage if he hasn't been already, so you know? **So we should be able to –**

Kathy/Sean/Jules – **Go, Jess, go!**

Jules (64) She's gainin' on 'em, look!

Sean (64) Fucking yes!

Jules Do it for Sheffield!

Kathy Watch her go, that's it my girl! Go on, girl, go on go on!

Sean She's in the lead –

Jules YES! Fucking –

Jules/Kathy YESSS!

Oh my god, I've pissed meself!

Celebration hugs.

Sean (*collapses on the sofa*) I need a lie down.

2012

Saturday 4th August (Evening)

Kathy (62) – *in her nurse's uniform – and* **Sean** *and* **Jules (64)** *are standing in front of the television, watching Jessica Ennis compete in the 800 metres of the London Olympics.*

Sean *and* **Jules** *have drinks – can of beer, glass of wine.*

Mike (42) – *also with a can – moves to the sofa, unseen by the others, and opens* **Kathy**'*s handbag.*

He removes notes from **Kathy**'*s handbag, as the others watch the race.*

Kathy / That's four gold medals she's got now! (*To* **Jules**.) Four gold medals, yer know I actually feel proud to be British for the first time in my life?

Jules Yer know Jessica Ennis went King Ecgbert's same as me?

Sean Now all we need is an end to austerity.

Kathy (*turning to* **Mike**) 'Ere, Mike, did yer / see that?

Mike (*pockets the notes, hands her the handbag*) / Yer handbag, look.

Kathy What?

Jules (*to* **Sean**, *watching TV*) She gets a gold medal, I get this lanky streak of Guinness.

Sean You can jump on my hurdle any night of the week.

Mike Aren't yer goin' to be late for / work? Yer handbag, don't forget yer handbag.

Kathy / Oh Christ, is that the time? – No yer right, Mike, thanks –

Sean (*of the TV*) George Osborne the Bullingdon coke-fiend. Boris the honey monster . . . – (*To* **Kathy**.) You're doing what, going into work?

Kathy (*to* **Jules**) Oh, I love you two, it's / just like the old days.

Sean / But I've only just fucking got here – (*To* **Mike**.) Remind yer mum it's Super Saturday. (*To* **Kathy**.) Super Saturday, Kath!

'Ere, Jules, are yer still alright to give me a lift? (*To* **Sean**.) I'm goin' into work now, Sean, but I'll see yer later, okay?

He'll keep an eye on him won't he, eh? Mike, I mean.

Mike / Want me to fetch anythin' from the shop when I / go?

Maya (10) *enters, dressed as Lord Voldemort* (*from Harry Potter*) *wielding her toy wand.*

Maya (*as she enters*) / Avada Kedavra! (*Hits* **Mike** *with the wand.*) Avada Kedavra, Uncle Mike!

Some laughter at **Maya** *as* **Rebecca (38)** *enters, holding* **Maya***'s jacket/bag.*

Rebecca (38) Alright Voldermort, it's past bedtime n' yer mum's havin' kittens.

Jules Need a lift, Rebecca?

Kathy You missed Jessica Ennis win 'er fourth gold just now.

Rebecca Who for, Great Britain? The same Great

Maya Arrr, can't I stay n' watch Usain Bolt? (*To* **Mike**.) Avada Kedavra!

Sean (*to* **Mike**) Lads together then, I guess.

Britain that supplies weapons to the IDF to kill Palestinian babies? (*To* **Maya**.) Come n' take yer jacket, Maya.

Mike 'Lads' right – what are yer, hunded n' eighty? (*Taking* **Maya**'*s wand*.) I'm goin' up the shop, anyone want anything from the shop?

Kathy Yer sister's at it again, Mike. – (*To* **Sean**.) Yer know I was just sayin', it's just like the old days, isn't it?

Rebecca Shove their gold medals up their –

Sean The old days are all I've got.

Mike *hits* **Rebecca** *with the wand*.

Kathy Keep an eye on 'im won't yer, please?

Rebecca 'Ey, gi'over, – (*Hits him*.) Spongin' twat. / Don't laugh, Maya.

Mike (*hits her*) / Avada Kedavra!

Hands the wand back to **Maya**, *with* –

Mike Course, I remember Duncan Goodhew n' Daley Thompson back in the eighties. Sat right 'ere, back when I were your age, me n' yer grandad. Back **when we still 'ad –**

Mike (*as he chops the coke*) **– somethin' to look forward to, yer remember that feelin'?** Back in the nineties, Sean, remember? Euro '96, Cool Britannia, pills every weekend.

Offers **Sean** *the note to snort the coke*.

Sean (*still coughing slightly*) No no, not –

Mike *snorts a line of coke*.

2012

Saturday 4th August (Late Night)

Mike *is chopping up cocaine on the table from a wrap. He has a rolled up five pound note.*

Sean *is semi-conscious on the sofa. Music on the stereo – "Loaded" by Primal Scream.*

Mike Back when birds were birds, when they weren't afraid to get their tits out.

Mike *chucks the note at* **Sean**, *then – as he rants – lights a cigarette.*

Mike Now it's all *X Factor* n' One Direction. Half the pubs shut down – good ones anyway.

Sean (*gives a 'thumbs up'*) Wetherspoons.

Mike Wetherspoons, yeah, n' if yer want a fag you have to stand out in the freezin' cold just so they can all protect themselves from passive smoking.

Mike *grabbing the rolled up note.*

Mike Everyone shit scared of goin' on tube, like – "Ooh, watch what yer say about . . . –

Sean *wretches/pukes, as* **Mike** *snorts another line.*

Mike (*cont.*) – . . . Islam, I don't want t'sound racist after he blows up my wife n' kids". I remember it were great when all we ever worried about was your lot. – I mean, who's –

Jules (64) *enters, carrying her car-keys.*

Mike (*cont.*) – worse eh, Sean? Beardy wahabi bastards blowin' up the high street or that fuck-wit Cameron shuttin' it all down? Pound shops everywhere, luxury flats sittin' empty where the brewery used to be.

Sean, *on his feet, pisses himself.*

Jules (*moves to* **Sean**) Oh Christ, Sean, not again. (*To* **Mike**.) You should know better, Mike, wait till yer mum gets 'ome.

Mike 'Ey, come on, we're only havin' a laugh. You lot used to stay up all night when we were kids.

Jules 'Ere, just give us an hand, will yer? (Pulls Sean off the floor.) Big stupid lump –

Mike Back of the net, Sean, yes!

Jules (*to* **Mike**) Funny yeah, have another line. **Yer know this isn't . . .**

Safiya (*retreating, with the hoover*) **– my idea of a good time,** Michael, soz.

2012

<u>Saturday August 11th (Daytime)</u>

It's hot and sunny.

The television is on– the women's volleyball.

Mike (*with a can of beer*) *pursues* **Safiya**, *the neighbour, who has just arrived, carrying a hoover.*

Mike (*following her, trying to take the hoover*) Alright, so just a little drink then, eh? Mo Farah's got the 5,000 metres tonight – he's Muslim like you.

Safiya Oh yeah, sounds magic.

Mike Magic hidden under that burkha, yer mean. We are neighbours after all, how about a little feel –

Safiya *whacks* **Mike** *across the face with the hoover nozzle – it really hurts – as* **Kathy** *enters – holding a can of furniture polish and a cloth.*

Safiya (*to* **Kathy**) Oh my god, I honestly dint mean –

Kathy That's alright, it's him what –

As she speaks, she moves to **Safiya**, *putting the furniture polish down, taking the hoover.*

Kathy – bust the Henry two days ago when 'e was rat-arsed anyway. Pay no attention, he's all mouth –

Mike (*to* **Safiya**) Pay no attention, yeah I'm practically invisible. – (*To* **Kathy**.) Piece o'shit were fallin' apart anyway – (*To* **Safiya**.) – 'Ey, did yer know my daughter's down there today? On the telly, look, right there –

Mike – *dazed – sits in front of the TV and the Olympics.*

Mike – Earls fuckin' Court, with 'er mum n' 'er new boyfriend.

Safiya (*to* **Kathy**, *making to leave*) It's fine, I'll pick it up tomorrow.

Safiya *exits to the hallway/front door.*

Mike, *alone in the room, sits down in front of the Olympics and drains the rest of his can.*

Mike Seven year old wonderin' where 'er dad is.

He searches for another cigarette, can't find one.

Mike *reaches for the can of furniture polish.*

He sprays the furniture polish into his mouth.

Until –

There is a knock at the front door, offstage.

Rajesh (59) (*off*) Come for the carpet, love, you in?

Second knock on the door.

Rajesh (*off*) Mrs Milner? Raj from Glenmill.

Kathy / Just a minute! (*To* **Safiya**.) Tomorrow? They should be done in an hour. 'Ere, let me –

Kathy *exits, following* **Safiya**.

Kathy (*off*) – see you out at least. – (*To* **Rajesh**.) Oh hello, Raj, sorry about that –

Rajesh (*off*) We alright to park there are we, love?

Kathy (*off*) Course yeah, I asked / next door to keep the space f'yer.

Rajesh (*off*) Just want to avoid a ticket, know what I mean, um . . .

Kathy (*off*) Kathy.

Rajesh (*off*) Kathy, great – we're / through here, are we?

Kathy / Free parkin' till the evenin' as far as I know – yeah, if yer just –

Kathy, **Rajesh** *and* **Shan** (**Raj***'s apprentice) as they enter the living room.* **Rajesh** *carries tools, and* **Shan** *carries a floor sander.* **Mike** *pockets the furniture polish.*

Kathy (*as she enters, cont.*) – mind all the bits o'crap all /over the floor.

Rajesh / Not a problem, love, this is paradise compared to –

The front door slams shut, off.

Rajesh (*cont.*) – most places we work round 'ere. – (*To* **Shan**.) I'd leave that in the hallway for the time bein', Shan, help me get this thing up first.

Shan Dust-masks?

Rajesh Dust-mask, yeah, reckon it's seen a bit of life. Grab me the large –

Shan *exits with the floor sander.*

Rajesh (*cont.*) – pliers while yer out there n'all. (*To* **Kathy**.) Good to see yer've made a start on this thanks, Kathy, it shouldn't take us too long–

Kathy (*to* **Mike**) What did you say to 'er? – 'Ey, go n' sober yerself up, we've got guests.

Pause.

Kathy Mike –

Mike / Women's volleyball.

Kathy Never mind that, make yerself useful.

Mike Women's volleyball. Japan versus South Korea.

Kathy Well, go on watch it in yer bedroom, Mike, this is settin' me back an entire month's wages no thanks to you. –

(*To* **Rajesh**.) What's that, love, sorry?

Rajesh Said it shouldn't take –

Kathy Normally right as rain with strangers, sorry. This one, he's like a dog on heat –

Kathy *kisses* **Mike***'s head.*

Rajesh Well, don't mind us, we'll be done in no time if yer want to carry on, um –

Shan *re-enters with the long pliers and dust-masks.*

Mike 'Ey, gi'oer, I'm not five!

Mike *reluctantly pulls himself from the floor, grabbing the can of furniture polish as he goes.*

Rajesh (*cont.*) – Magic, Shan, great. – (*To* **Kathy**.) Seen a bit of life, like?

Kathy Seen a bit of life, yeah. About twenty-five years' worth I think.

Rajesh (*signals to* **Shan** *who moves to carpet with the pliers*) Blimey, right, / twenty-five years.

Kathy / Longer maybe, I don't know. Bucks Fizz were still in the charts.

Mike *exits with the polish.*

Rajesh Bucks Fizz? I've got a bunch of C45 cassette-tapes in the van if yer want to feel old. Cat Stevens, Neil Sedaka –

Kathy Aren't you more Vera Lynn?

Rajesh Fifty-nine, my love, sixty next month. Twice married, twice divorced – kids've all fucked off so there's just me n' this slaphead against the world. – 'Ere, mind yer trotters a sec, let's –

Rajesh *joins* **Shan** (*with the pliers*) *to start on the carpet.*

Rajesh – see the damage. Who nailed this down, yer husband?

Kathy Maybe, yeah, it's just me n' 'im –

Rajesh (*to* **Shan**) / Grab the stanley, we'll do it in sections.

Kathy *picks* **Brian**'s *urn, then immediately puts it down.*

Kathy (*as she does so*) – n' a ward full of terminals these days. Can't say I get out much.

Rajesh (*pulling at the edges of the carpet*) That's no good, a beautiful young woman.

Kathy Oh shuddup, I'd hardly say –

Rajesh Say what I like, I know what I see. What's point of a new carpet if yer've got no one to roll on it with, eh? (*He sings the opening line of Oasis' "Roll With It".*) Don't treat yerself, the next thing yer know **it'll be Christmas n'there –**

2012

<u>Tuesday 18th (Early Morning)</u>

Mike*'s been up all night. He speaks on the landline.*

Mike **– still processin' it for** fucksake. Income support, Nina, it's complex. . . . I said it's a complex process these days, it's due any day now. . . . Course I'll pay yer back, yer know I'll pay yer back. For the kids, yeah, for Christmas, I'm . . . (*Hits the phone against his head.*) – fuckin' tryin' aren't I?! . . . Alright, look, listen . . .

Sits on the floor. As he speaks on the phone, he pulls a wrap of cocaine from his pocket and starts to open it to take a dab.

Mike – Listen listen, just another twenty quid or somert then, eh? Twenty quid n'then in one more week I **promise I'll 'ave –**

2012

<u>Monday December 24th (Early Evening)</u>

Christmas tree, decorations.

Carol service on the TV.

Kathy, *slumped on the sofa, watches on as a very drunk/ coked-up* **Mike** (*wearing toy 'reindeer' Alice band*) *crouches over a box of* **Brian***'s old vinyl records on the floor.*

Mike **– an original Sgt Pepper,** I know there is, 'e used to play it all the time.

Kathy Okay, Mike, / if you insist –

Mike / An original 1967 Sgt Pepper, yer must've seen it. Must be worth two hundred or more at least.

Kathy How about I just transfer some money into yer account?

Mike Marvin Gaye at least though, look, that'll fetch fifty quid.

He drinks from a can or bottle, and has a plastic bag for the records he selects.

Kathy Yer'll never sell it on Christmas Eve, the shops are goin' to be closed in half / an hour.

Mike Well, are yer goin' to help me or not? (*Flicking through the records.*) Shit-tons o' Genesis.

Leonard Cohen. –

Finds a 'Dark Side of the Moon' LP (the one from scene '1974').

Mike Dark Side, bingo.

Mike *starts bagging it up with the others in the plastic bag.*

Mike Original Dark Side, look –

Kathy I know, I bought it for him. 1974 –

Mike Probably never even played it since. They'll bite my 'and off at Rare n' Racy, I bet. Fuckin' buy my own sniff for once.

Kathy Yeah –

Mike Buy my own sniff without you sat there pullin' that disgustin' old woman's face.

Pause – **Mike** *climbs to his feet, with the can/bottle and bag of records.*

Mike Well?

Kathy Well, what? Well, nothin', –

Mike Well, don't get too fuckin' excited, Mum, it's not like 'e's here. It's not like he's sat up on a cloud with a big fat spliff in 'is 'and lookin' down.

Kathy Alright, yer paint / a very vivid picture –

Mike / Fuckin' nowhere, Mum, geddit? Get that into yer thick 'ead.

Mike *picks up the urn.*

Stuck on the sideboard like someone's idea of sick joke. Like 'e weren't a joke to begin with. Yer know if you 'ad half a brain in yer 'ead, yer would've kicked 'im out the house years ago.

Mike *empties* **Brian**'s *ashes onto the new carpet.*

Mike There. What yer got to say to me now, eh, Mum? New fuckin' carpet, that curryman's new carpet, look. Yer still goin' to put some money in my account?

Pause.

Well, yer'd better. Two days time from now, yer'd better –

Kathy *exits.*

Mike – put another couple of hundred in. The fuckin' least you can do.

Pause.

Mike (*calls*) Right, Mum?

Mike *takes a drink from his can.*

He rubs his foot/trainer on the pile of ashes, then lifts his foot to look at the sole of his trainers.

Kathy *re-enters with a dustpan and brush.*

Mike *watches as* **Kathy** *crouches and starts sweeping up the ashes.*

Long pause.

Mike Yer know yer can speak.

Pause.

Fuckin' say somert, this is your house, what yer given me / the silent treatment for?

Kathy Alright, just stop it, **Mike, stop –**

Rebecca (39) **– cryin' now, Maya, sssh,** yer'll be fine, we'll be fine won't we, mum?

2013

Monday April 8th
(Afternoon)

Kathy (63) Easter holidays soon.

Maya (11) Please don't tell anyone. Don't call the school again. Miss Monet –

Rebecca Wasn't Miss Monet there when it happened?

Maya No, I dunno –

Kathy (63) *with* **Maya (11)** *who is just back from school. In her uniform, she's been visibly fighting.*

BBC News on the TV reporting the death of Margaret Thatcher.

Kathy No one's callin' the school, don't worry.

Rebecca Who said what to yer exactly? I've told yer before yer've got to / speak to Miss Monet.

Maya Everyone, Mum! Like "What's it like livin' wi'two lesbians, Maya? Were yer real parents gay?"

Kathy Ignore them, they're just jealous.

Rebecca Alright Mum, thanks – look, why don't yer / put the kettle on or somert?

Kathy / Was it that Chantelle again, love?

Maya Chantelle *and* Shaniqua, they put my sports day photos up on Instagram. (*To* **Rebecca**.) The one / where it's rainin' –

Kathy That's 'cause they're jealous, bullies are always / jealous.

Maya I dint even know how they got 'em! Like how did they unlock my phone? Shaniqua were tryin' to get me to go up Concorde Park t'say sorry until I found out there were a whole gang of 'em waitin' there. Some roadman I don't even know held me on the floor n'made me say I were ISIS.

Rebecca / Alright, Mum, don't give 'em excuses.

Kathy Who's makin' excuses?

Rebecca Stay out of it if yer've got nothin' useful to say. Who's Chantelle?

Rebecca Who called you ISIS? Why've I never heard o'this Chantelle?

Kathy Yes, and the best thing you can do is ignore them. Secondary school / starts in September, Maya, remember?

Rebecca / For Christ's sake, Mum! – (*To* **Maya**.) Look, we're goin' to do this properly, alright? I'm goin' to speak to Melissa n'we're going to talk to Miss Monet first thing, and if she won't deal with it then I'll talk to Chantelle's parents myself. 'Ey, come on now, ssssh (*Strokes and cuddles* **Maya**.) – we'll sort this together, eh?

Kathy *makes to leave the room, with –*

Kathy Ignore them n'they'll get their comeuppance soon enough. Yer think (*Gestures to the TV.*) Margaret Thatcher didn't get what she deserved in the end?

Kathy *exits, as* **Rebecca** *cuddles a crying* **Maya**.

Kathy (*off*) Dead in some hotel room in her eighties. Yer know yer big Uncle Mike were just the same **when 'e were –**

2013

Thursday May 30th (Early Evening)

Kathy *is on her mobile, mid-call.*

The doorbell rings.

Kathy (*on the mobile*) **– forty three, yeah,** Michael Milne. . . . No, I'm not sure, that's why I'm callin'. I just thought 'e might've turned up at your hostel . . . Yes, I understand that. Yer a homeless charity, I get it, yer don't 'ave to . . . – Well, I don't know where 'e is, that's what I'm –

Kathy (*cont., on the mobile*) – sayin' . . . – No, I've done that already – Look, sorry, can yer just bear with me, love, please? I've got the carpet man comin' to mend me boiler, –

Kathy *moves and makes to call upstairs.*

Kathy (*cont., on the phone*) – I just need to . . . – (*Calls.*) 'Ere Maya, come down a second will yer, love? – (*Back on the phone.*) No, I have called 101 . . . About five months now. Roughly five months, since Christmas . . . No, the –

Doorbell rings again. She exits.

Kathy (*cont., off*) – police don't seem concerned at all if I'm perfectly honest. (*Calls up.*) Get the door for me, Maya, please! How long's that shower takin' yer? – (*Back on phone.*) They said it's probably nothin'. Said 'e'll probably just turn up when 'e's –

She sees **Maya** *in the living room doorway.* **Maya** *has her school shirt sleeves rolled up. She holds a pair of scissors. She has cut one of her arms.*

Kathy Oh, Maya, no –

Maya I'm sorry, I tried.

Kathy Maya, no. No, your / beautiful arms –

Maya / I tried but it hurt. I don't think I were doin' it right.

Kathy / Well of course it hurts! Doin' what right?!

Maya On the video Chantelle showed us, it wasn't meant to start / drippin' everywhere –

Kathy Is that what yer've been doin' up there all this time?! I thought yer were in the shower.

Kathy Don't tell me mum, will yer?

The doorbell rings again.

Maya Please, Gran, she'll have kittens if / she sees me –

Kathy / 'Ere, give me those bloody / scissors will yer?! For fucksake, the boiler man –

Maya Well yer don't have t'shout at me, / do yer? I tried ignorin' them like yer said.

Kathy No one's shoutin' at yer, / Maya – Ignorin' who, sorry? Don't put this on me.

Maya Yes you are, yer meant to be on my side n' now yer / just shoutin' –

Kathy – I am not shoutin', I am not shoutin'! Oh Christ, oh **fuckin' 'ell –**

Rajesh (61) (*on entering, in the dark*) – **fire,**

Kaz, yer scared me then.

Pause.

Rajesh (*in the dark*) Kaz.

Pause.

Rajesh (*in the dark*) 'Ey, Kaz –

2014

<u>Tuesday October 14th (2.00 am)</u>

The lights are off.

Kathy (64) – *in her dressing gown – is looking out the window, as –*

Rajesh (61) *has just entered in his boxers and t-shirt.*

Kathy (*in the dark*) It's Kathy, gi'over callin' me that.

Rajesh (*in the dark*) Why? It's yer name, int it?

Kathy (*in the dark*) Make me sound like a Shane Meadows film. "Kaz."

Rajesh (*in the dark*) Oh I'm sorry, Audrey Hepburn, d'yer want more diamonds with yer peacock soup?

Kathy (*in the dark*) Funny, yeah, / Hurdy Gurdy.

Rajesh (*in the dark*) / Funny, yeah, like comin' down to find you sat in the dark at three in the mornin'. Yer find a pea under the mattress or somert?

Kathy (*in the dark*) Couldn't bear your snorin' more like. Like sharin' a bed with Chewbacca.

Rajesh (*in the dark*) 'Ey, take that back, Grandma, it's you what needs 'er sinus drained.

Kathy (*laughs*) Sorry, what did you just call me? / Who the hell's grandma?

Rajesh (*laughs*) / Well, it's true int it? (*Then sings.*) – "Grandma, we love you, Grandma, we do" –

Rajesh *turns the main light on.*

Kathy – Oh my god – blind me, Raj!

Rajesh *giggles, flicks the main light off and on – like a strobe light.*

Kathy Fucksake, turn it off will yer?

As he flicks the switch, **Rajesh** *raps the fifth/sixth line of The Sugarhill Gang's "Rapper's Delight".*

Kathy Yer'll give yerself a shock yer carry on. That's all I need, you lyin' there stiff as a board.

Rajesh (*drapes over her*) Thought yer liked me stiff as a board.

Kathy Oh dear god . . . – (*Pushes him off.*) It's two o'clock in the mornin'.

Rajesh *kisses/bites* **Kathy***'s neck.*

Kathy (*laughs*) Stop it will yer? Someone'll see!

Rajesh Who, the man in the moon? (*Howls like a wolf.*) Ow-ow-owwww!

Kathy Fuck off, Raj, don't. Yer think yer charmin' but yer not.

Rajesh Wow, alright, that's me told.

Kathy Why's everythin' have to be a joke wi'you? Freddie Starr.

Rajesh (*laughs*) Freddie friggin' Starr? Richard Pryor more like. Bill Hicks.

Kathy Who?

Rajesh Well if yer'd ever let me bring round the DVD. (*Mimics Bill Hicks.*) "Life is only a dream and we are an imitation of ourselves."

He puts his hands on her back, her neck – massaging her.

Pause.

Rajesh Ignore me, sorry, I'm a Class A dick. Maybe I should just –

Kathy Lower down.

Rajesh Eh?

Kathy Lower down.

Rajesh Oh –

Kathy T'the right a bit, there.

Rajesh *leans closer, massaging.*

Rajesh Bit colonial, this int it, eh?

Kathy *and* **Rajesh** *laugh, then kiss.*

Long pause, as the kiss, move down onto the floor.

Then **Kathy** *pulls away.*

Kathy Sorry –

Rajesh No, it's / alright –

Kathy God, I'm sorry. Shit.

Rajesh Yer sure yer alright?

Kathy Yeah no, get on with it.

Rajesh (*laughs*) What? Talk about gettin' me in the mood.

Kathy No, just . . .

Kathy *puts her legs round* **Rajesh***'s waist.*

Rajesh Oh! Like that, yer mean?

Kathy Like that or somert, yeah. Shit . . .

Rajesh Great, yeah.

Kathy Oh shit shit shit. Oh god, okay . . .

Rajesh *and* **Kathy** *slowly make love.*

Kathy Right, good-oh then.

Rajesh Yeah?

Kathy Good-oh then, yep. No, wait, . . . –

Rajesh I can slow / down again.

Kathy / Slow down again, yeah. No, wait, fuck. Fuck shit . . .

Kathy *pulls herself free.*

Kathy . . . sorry.

Rajesh No, that's fine.

Kathy It's me, it's all me –

Rajesh I said it's fine alright, don't . . . –

Kathy Too soon or somert maybe. Sorry.

Rajesh Will yer stop sayin' sorry a minute?

Pause, as **Kathy** *pulls her dressing gown back on.*

Kathy Shit.

Kathy *wipes the tears from her eyes.*

Long pause.

Been awhile, yer know? Since before Brian got sick even . . . – Over ten years or more.

Rajesh Well, yer'd never tell –

Kathy Obviously a bit rusty –

Rajesh What if I happen to like rusty? Rusty's good. I'm like the Tin Man's older brother, me.

Kathy Right, so what's that make me, fuckin' Dorothy?

Rajesh *moves and grabs an unfinished spliff from the ashtray.*

He lights it and takes a couple of puffs.

Rajesh Felt perfect to me.

Pause.

Rajesh *hands the spliff to* **Kathy**.

Kathy *hesitates, then takes it.*

Kathy (*as she does so*) Hurdy Gurdy.

Rajesh Oh right, like the Donovan song?

Kathy I dunno, yeah, probably. Somethin' way back now. Swingin' Blue Jeans.

Kathy *smokes the spliff.*

Grow up centre of the world, don't yer? Hit puberty n'yer want to get as far away from the world as possible. Turn sixteen n' you think yer can change the world. Spend yer twenties n'thirties in a daze, gradually ground down by the crushin' reality that yer no different to yer parents. Turn forty n' out of nowhere yer past it. Desperate to be noticed, to remind people 'yes, I do actually exist'. Turn fifty n' yer can barely look in the mirror. Years feel like weeks, the HRT kicks in. Fifty turns to sixty and then it's anyone's guess what the fuck you are. Potterin' around tryin' not to kill everyone.

Kathy *hands the spliff back to* **Rajesh**.

Rajesh You should watch more shit TV.

Kathy Eh?

Rajesh Shit TV's the answer, I'm tellin' yer. *First Dates*, *Gogglebox*, *The Only Way is Essex*. No wonder yer feel shit about yerself with all those poncey books yer've got around the 'ouse, fillin' yer head with words. Should let me take care o'yer.

Kathy Unpaid employee of the heterosexual male?

Rajesh What?

Kathy No, nothin'.

Kathy *shuts the curtains and moves to* **Rajesh**.

Kathy Hope yer not plannin' on goin' into work tomorrow mornin'.

She starts to remove his t-shirt.

Kathy Don't imagine yer'll be much use **drivin' that van after –**

2015

Saturday October 3rd (Evening)

Mark Ronson's "Uptown Funk" playing at low volume on the TV.

Kathy (65) *is on her mobile phone, holding a posh happy retirement card.*

A plastic bag, hung on her arm, full of other cards and presents, including a Game of Thrones box set, which she struggles – as she speaks – to unload.

Kathy (*reads from card. On phone*) **– ". . . forty years** working as a staff nurse in the NHS. You should know that this is a tremendous achievement and, on behalf of all the staff at the Northern General, I'd like to wish you all the best on your retirement. You have had . . ." – Yeah, I know it's bollocks, Rob, yer not tellin' me anythin' I don't know already.–

As she speaks – **Rajesh** *enters, with a bottle of champagne and two glasses. Over the next, he dances and pours the drinks.*

Kathy (65) (*cont., on the phone*) Cut n'paste job, I know – (*Reads from the card.*) "Your retirement will be a loss to the nursing profession." – Exactly yeah, what profession?

Jeremy Hunt sellin' us off to the highest bidder. Island of care in a country that's stopped carin'.

Kathy *takes her glass, drinking as she speaks. As* **Rajesh (62)** *kisses her ears and slides his hand down the front of her top, as. –*

Kathy (*on the phone, cont.*) – Well, I don't know, Brian, people only seem to sit up n'take notice if David Cameron's shagged a pig or not. When it comes to real life, to things that actually matter. **When people decide they want –**

2016

Thursday June 23rd (Evening)

Kathy, **Sean**, **Jules** *and* **Rajesh** *are drinking and smoking and watching the BBC coverage of the European Referendum results.*

There are remains of a Chinese takeaway.

Sean (68) **– a vote to leave the European Union because** they're as thick as fuckin' pig shit.

Kathy (66) (*laughing*) Oh, come on, Sean, give them some credit –

Jules (68) Who, the great British electorate?

Sean Oh, they know how to lose at penalties the chips-with-everything cunts, I'll give 'em that. Here's an idea, let's destroy our own livelihoods because we don't like Albanians or brown people.

Rajesh (63) Two world wars –

Sean (*laughs*) Two world wars and a German queen – we demand our sovereignty, you hear?

Sean *playfully grabs* **Rajesh** *by the collar.*

Sean (*as he does so*) You 'ear me, son? This is our country and we demand our fucking –

Sean *starts coughing, lets go of* **Rajesh**.

Jules Christ, Sean, put your hand over your mouth.

Sean Nigel Farage looking like he's auditioning for some community hall production of *Toad of Toad Hall*. Tweedle-Gove and Tweedle-Johnson giving it "the wheels on the bus".

Kathy Alice in Brexit-land. Have another vodka, Sean, come on –

Kathy *hands* **Sean** *the bottle of vodka.*

Rajesh "First they come for the Jews, then they come for the blacks, the transgender hezbollahs –"

Sean (*pouring the vodka*) I swear to god, my doctor's going to kill me, Jules, my fucking kidneys.

Kathy What are they on now, 55 per cent?

Jules I've got a pack of Day Nurse somewhere.

Rajesh Well, it certainly looks that way. Takin' back control.

Sean Dimbleby, you Tory! Taking control of what – the fisheries?

Rajesh Not even the fishermen understand the fisheries.

Sean Yeah, it's like every provincial Joe and Ethel has a degree in Agricultural Economics now. Sat in the pub complaining about Brussels when they couldn't even point to it on a map.

Jules Good old empirical racism coming back to haunt us.

Rajesh Not that it ever went away.

Kathy Anyone want this egg fried rice?

Sean (*to* **Kathy**) And this is something your friend Jeremy Corbyn needs to learn. He can't just pull a Tardis out 'is arse and take us back to the Jarrow Crusades. The man's got too much faith in people. He needs to wake up and see that the world's moved on, that you don't have to be rich to be a cunt.

Jules He'd make a good Doctor Who.

Sean He'd make a shit Doctor Who, have you heard the way he breathes?

Kathy He believes in equality, the living wage. And he's preferable to Farage.

Sean My left ballbag's preferable to Farage. You see this ballbag? This sixty-eight-year-old ballbag's going to be on the first Aer Lingus home if that tweed-wearing sociopath gets anywhere near Number 10. God bless and good luck.

Kathy Okay –

Sean Okay?

Kathy I said okay – /

Jules She said okay.

Sean Okay, well try and contain yourself, Kathy, you know it's only been forty years.

Jules And forty years ago you didn't want to anythin' to do with the Common Market.

Sean Right, because it was forty fucking years before a global descent into neoliberalism. Before Facebook came along and turned us into a nation of amchair experts on issues we didn't know existed. Did anyone give two shits about the EU until a couple of months ago? Last I heard we were tying ourselves in knots over Jimmy Savile.

Rajesh Yer should listen to BBC Asian Network, pal.

Sean Face it, you boys love a partition.

Jules People want change, they want real change.

Kathy Christ, did I just 'ave a flashback to 1969?

Sean Flashbacks, right – you can count me in there. Driving down the M1 with a pocket full of quaaludes. (*To* **Jules**.) Kathy and Brian in the back of your camper van. (*To*

Kathy.) "You're the most beautiful girl this side of Sheaf Market, have you ever read *The Naked Lunch*?"

Kathy Except I was up the duff with Mike.

Sean You were never up the duff.

Kathy The summer of '69? I think I'd remember.

Rajesh Yeah, dickhead, you think she'd remember.

Jules And since when did I have a camper van? I never had a friggin' / camper van –

Sean *starts coughing.*

Sean (*as he coughs*) Sorry no, ignore me, sorry . . . –

Sean *stumbles to his feet, making for the door, as he coughs/ struggles for breath.*

Jules It was Roy Mather's van, you were out of it. Uppers or downers or whatever else you were peddlin'.

Sean Well, whatever it took to win your heart, my love. Whatever it took to beat the system. (*To* **Rajesh**.) Ha, and see how that turned out? My great-grandfather devotes everything to liberating the South of Ireland, all I've got's a pair of Next jeans and a senior citizen's rail card. I mean, fuck life really.

Rajesh Try bein' brown for a day.

Jules Try bein' an educated woman.

Kathy No, I wasn't up the duff, yer right! I'd only just met Brian when we drove down t'London. We'd only been together a couple of months, I was still at college.

Sean Hangin' onto his arm, with him completely oblivious. Christ, I wish he was here now.

Kathy He wasn't oblivious, he was actually very charmin'.

Sean Right, and then you gave it all up to be his maid.

Kathy Excuse me, sorry?

Sean Ah dream on, Kathy, yer've been a maid your entire life. – (*To* **Raj**.) The point is there'll never be a revolution in our lifetime. Not while there's Netflix to keep us distracted, not while . . .

He coughs violently, hanging onto the door.

Sean . . . we're shot of this lot anyway, fucking – (*Coughs.*) – Rupert Murdoch or whoever. Once we've done away with the whole . . . (*Catching breath.*)

Jules Christ, Sean, are you alright?

Sean The whole right wing fucking media, right?! – I mean, who are we supposed to trust anymore, are you with me?! People people people like –

Sean *wheezes sharply – collapses/crashes onto the ground.*

Kathy Oh my god –

Sean *spasms, deep painful gasps – fighting for air.*

Rajesh What the 'ell's wrong with 'im? /

Jules Sean, fuckin' 'ell!

Kathy *and* **Jules** *rush over to him –* **Jules** *tries to grab him, pull him up.*

Kathy Don't grab at 'im, stop!

Jules *tries again, but* **Kathy** *slaps her away.*

Kathy What did I tell / yer, Jules?

Jules / For godsake, help him!

Sean *gasps/spasms, clutching his chest.* **Rajesh** *backs off.*

Kathy Hey Sean, come on, love . . . – /

Jules Oh god.

Kathy *rolls him over on his back.*

Kathy Come on now, breathe. Breathe, Sean, you can do it . . .

Sean *spasms, stops breathing.*

Kathy Oh shit . . . –

Kathy *performs CPR, pushing hard and fast on* **Sean***'s chest.*

Kathy Shit, come on now –

Jules What d'yer mean 'shit', what's wrong?!

Kathy Come on now, breathe.

Jules Breathe, Sean, breathe!

Jules Oh god, oh god – (*To* **Rajesh**.) The hell are yer standin' there for?! Do somethin', wanker, call the –

Jules *shoves* **Rajesh**

Jules – ambulance will yer?!

Jules *returns to* **Kathy** *and* **Sean**, *as* **Rajesh** *frantically searches through his pockets, looking for his mobile phone.*

Kathy *performs the CPR, performing mouth-to-mouth rescue breaths.*

Rajesh (*can't find phone*) Sorry, love, I can't . . .

Jules Use the bloody landline then!

Rajesh Oh . . .

Jules In the hall! The landline in the hall!

Rajesh *rushes out, exits.*

Kathy *performs CPR.*

Jules Oh god, Sean, not now. Not now, my baby. . .

Jules *holds* **Sean***'s hand as* **Kathy** *performs rescue breaths.*

The sound of the referendum results show on the TV, as . . .

Kathy *performs CPR.*

She performs rescue breaths.

Kathy *performs CPR, then . . .*

Slows down, stops.

Looks at **Sean***, feels his neck pulse.*

He's gone.

Pause.

She makes to perform CPR again, but . . .

Stops.

She looks to **Jules***, shakes her head.*

Gets up, makes way for **Jules***, who . . .*

. . . clumsily grabs and embraces **Sean***, sobbing.*

Kathy *climbs and slumps onto the sofa, exhausted.*

The sound of the Referendum and **Jules***'s sobbing/groans.*

Long pause.

Kathy (*calls*) Raj?

Pause.

Can yer turn the heatin' off for me, please?

Pause.

We need to turn the heatin' off. Raj, love, can yer run t'the boiler for me? **We need to keep his body cool . . . we need to keep 'im cool before –**

Rebecca (43) – **Donald Trump assaults another** woman then boasts about it on social media. What kind of message does that send out?

Pause.

Rebecca Mum . . .

Kathy (67) No, Becs, yer right –

Rebecca So that kind of behaviour's acceptable now. I dunno, maybe we should all feel privileged to be groped by someone like him with all his money n' power?

Kathy I'm not arguin'.

Rebecca Not to mention the blatant racism, the Islamophobia – you've seen his Tweets.

Pause.

Mum, for fucksake –

Kathy Don't follow 'im then.

Rebecca A reaction would be nice.

Kathy I'm givin' you a reaction.

Rebecca An *appropriate* reaction. A bit of anger or passion.

Kathy What, so yer'd like me to start rantin' n' ravin' for no reason? It's very simple, Rebecca, stay off Twitter if 'e's windin' you up.

2017

Saturday 21st January (Morning)

Kathy (67) *is on the sofa, doing the* Guardian *crossword.*

Saturday Kitchen is on TV.

She has a sling on her arm for a strained arm/wrist

Rebecca (43) *is stood near the living room door, with a travel bag and a placard that says "WE SHOULD ALL BE FEMINISTS".*

She wears a stripey hat.

As she speaks, she places the placard with the others – one that says "WHO RUNS THE WORLD?", another that says "CAN'T COMB OVER MISOGYNY" – that are leant against the wall, by the living room door.

Rebecca You've got grandkids, haven't yer? What about Maya and Alice or Lucas even? If that's the sort of man they've got to look up to –

Kathy He's not the only man in the world.

Rebecca He's President of the United States.

Kathy Only just.

Rebecca What?

Kathy Look, I'm a lot older than you –

Rebecca I'm forty fuckin' three.

Kathy Well, he's only just got the job, love.

Rebecca Who?

Kathy Trump, he's got four whole years still, maybe he'll turn things around if yer give him a chance.

Rebecca Are you serious? Oh / my god.

Kathy / There's got to be some reason people voted for 'im, they can't all be Ku Klux Klan. You don't live in America, it might feel very different there. Maybe people are just tired of the same old same old.

Rebecca He's on tape boastin' about grabbin' young girls.

Kathy You asked for a response, I'm givin' you one. Yer can't judge everyone by what they happen to do in private, Becs, imagine if I'd done that with you.

Pause.

Kathy Sorry, no, yer know I didn't mean that.

Rebecca Now I know where Mike gets it.

Kathy Oh give over, Becs, yer know that's not what / I meant.

Rebecca / Like jumpin' into bed with the bloke from the carpet shop? That kind of private?

Kathy Well, yer needn't worry about 'im. –

Rebecca I'm not worried, I'm mortified.

Kathy And 'e's not just 'some bloke' –

Rebecca Is that why yer've decided to not to come today? / Sprucin' the place up for yer fancy man.

Kathy / What? No, of course not, don't be stupid. 'Fancy man' – we haven't seen each other in months.

Rebecca Three weeks plannin', hotels booked. D'yer know how much it cost us to book three adjacent rooms within walkin' distance of Trafalgar Square?

Kathy Yes, n'I've broken my bloody wrist, I'm not supposed to / go anywhere –

Rebecca / It's not broken, it's sprained and I know you've been hooverin'.

Kathy I've what?

Rebecca In the hall, yer can see the hoover trails.

Kathy Oh, well alert the village elders –

Rebecca Rather sit there bingin' on *Game of Thrones* while we're down Hyde Park tryin' to make our voices heard. I've told you who's goin' to be there, haven't I? Yvette Cooper, Stella Creasey.

Kathy All the big names, Rebecca, yeah. – Christ, don't you ever get tired?

Rebecca Exhausted, Kath, frankly. Melissa's already down there, she's expectin' us at three o'clock. Helen n' Jo are goin' to be 'ere any minute with the van.

Kathy Who the hell's Helen n' Jo? I've never even / heard of Helen n' Jo.

Rebecca They're friends of Melissa's.

Kathy So why isn't / Melissa here? Too good for us?

Rebecca / Friends of Melissa's from the life drawing class, it's their van, we've been over this, / read back over yer texts.

Kathy N' I suppose Melissa took the train like a normal person, did she? Look, I'm not rattlin' around in the back of some other new life-drawing lesbian's van all weekend, Becca, sorry, not with my wrist.

Rebecca Yer said yer wanted to come.

Kathy Yeah, when I bumped into you on Fargate the other day. I didn't think yer'd be on the phone to the Premier Inn the moment I turned onto Chapel Walk. Fartin' around with a placard at nearly sixty-eight years old, fuckin' arthritis in my left knee –

Rebecca So do some yoga like I showed –

Kathy I don't need yoga, I just want t'finish my crossword. And I'm sorry yer don't like that misogynistic overgrown Cheeto who's sittin' in the White House, but that's democracy.

Rebecca What?

Kathy That's democracy.

Rebecca Oh, come on, / listen to yerself –

Kathy The right to vote – that's what real feminists fought for all those years ago. Bunch o'ridiculous placards that make no sense – why haven't yer put 'em by the front door like I asked?

Kathy *grabs a couple of the placards and makes to exit.*

Kathy (*as she does so*) Splinters n'mud all over my good clean floor.

Rebecca Yeah, 'cause that's the important thing –

Kathy It is important, I live 'ere.

Kathy *exits with the placards. Over the next,* **Rebecca** *picks up the paper/crossword.*

Kathy (*off*) Carryin' on when I just want t'finish my crossword in peace. When yer've got an fifteen-year-old daughter at home.

Rebecca Maya's fine, don't bring Maya into this.

Kathy (*off*) Small wonder she bodged-up 'er exams with you gallivantin' round the world like Willy Fog.

Rebecca She didn't bodge-up anythin', they were the end of year mocks. No one cares about end of year mocks.

Kathy *re-enters, looks around for her newspaper, with –*

Kathy (*entering*) Except when it comes to predictive grades. When it comes to choosin' 'er A levels –

Rebecca Maya's a smart, secure, intelligent young woman, and she's already got an offer from High Storrs.

Kathy Oh, and suppose it'll me who's footin' the bill for all 'er fees n'accomodation then will it, eh? All yer dramarama for bugger-all money –

Rebecca Oh, here she goes.

Kathy What?

Rebecca Yer doin' it again. Stop changin' the subject, / Mum, yer know yer don't pay fees.

Kathy Doin' what again?

Rebecca (*passes her the newspaper*) Void.

Kathy What?

Rebecca Blank space, four letters. Void.

Kathy *grabs the newspaper, inspects the crossword.*

Rebecca Creative therapy, Mum, not dramarama.

Kathy Yeah, for bog-all money.

Rebecca I'm not in it for the money. There's kids in some of the poorest places in the world who've had their lives turned around by the work we've done –

Kathy Like Maya, yer mean? Carvin' 'er arms up for weeks on end–

Rebecca And Maya were only two-year-old when she left Beirut – scared shitless, not a word of English. I think I've done pretty well considerin'.

Kathy Okay . . .

Rebecca Look, I'm not sixteen anymore, I actually believe in what I'm doin'.

Pause.

Rebecca Mum –

Kathy No no no, ignore me.

Rebecca This is important to me.

Kathy I know it is, yer don't have to shove / it in my face.

Rebecca Shove it in your face, what am I shovin' in yer face? / For fucksake, Mum –

Kathy Look, I'm proud of yer, Rebecca, what else d'yer want me to say?

Rebecca Then how come whenever I try to to tell yer about it, yer make me feel like I'm tryin' to show off? I'm not tryin' to show off, I'm just –

Kathy Doin' what you need to do, / Rebecca, it's fine.

Rebecca – / tryin' to involve you in my life because I thought you might be interested, but if yer not interested –

Kathy I never said I wasn't interested –

Rebecca – then the next time yer try tellin' me about somethin' you've done, I'll just nod my 'ead n' change the subject like you do, shall I? One of yer neighbours wins a tenner on the lottery and it's the biggest thing that's ever happened. I tell yer I've been interrogated by Israeli forces for eight hours straight or that we nearly had our car ambushed over in Lagos and it's like "Oh, really? There was a three-legged dog in the park this mornin'".

Kathy Which three-legged dog?

Rebecca Constantly ignored or put down or taken the piss out of – like, "Who the hell does she think she is? Don't start thinkin' yer any better than us back 'ome, Rebecca" – and I've never once thought that. And I'm sorry if what I do in my work makes you uncomfortable, but I genuinely thought yer might be interested and I genuinely genuinely want you in my life, but if this the sum total of what you're going to give me in return, then it's probably better for my own mental health that I'm not.

Rebecca *gets her things together, puts her jacket on.*

Thought yer might've welcomed gettin' out the house for the day.

Pause – she gets her rucksack together.

Thought yer might've been a bit more –

A van horn honks outside.

– adventurous once you retired if we're bein' honest.

Kathy Well, sorry to disappoint you, Rebecca, / we can't all be Indiana Jones.

Rebecca Go travellin' or somethin' – no, not Indiana Jones, Mum, yer know that's / not what I mean.

Kathy / And who's goin' to look after Maya while I'm down the Temple of Doom?

Rebecca A fuckin' city break or somethin'. Paris or Venice. You used to talk about Venice all the time when we were kids. Maya's fifteen, yer don't have to worry about 'er. Lazin' around on that armchair week after week in front of the telly –

Kathy Oh, so forty year workin' every shift I could get at the Northern General wasn't enough? Cookin' n'cleanin' n' keepin' the house presentable –

Rebecca Oh shut up, that were dad, it was always dad. You were never even there, Mum –

Kathy Oh that's right, blame the woman again. Everyone blames the woman.

The van horn honks outside.

Pause.

Rebecca I'll tell Melissa yer hurt yer wrist.

Rebecca *exits, carrying her bag and her placard.*

The front door is heard shutting.

Kathy *picks up her crossword and pen.*

Pause.

She puts the crossword and pen down, and takes the TV remote control.

Turns on the News, Donald Trump making a victory speech to his supporters.

Kathy *watches the report, then . . .*

The sound of the van engine revving up, outside.

Kathy *gets up, makes to exit.*

Kathy (*as she leaves*) Becs. Rebecca, love.

She exits.

Kathy Rebecca, wait. **Just hold on a minute will yer, love, I'm –**

Kathy (68) (*as she enters*) **– in the hallway, yer can leave** it 'ere, Jules, thanks.

Kathy *tries turning the lightswitch on, but it's not working.*

Kathy Ah, damn it – (*to* **Jules**) Just dump it in the hall there, it's alright.

Jules (*as she enters*) Bulb not workin'?

2018

<u>Thursday January 4th (Evening)</u>

It's dark, the lights are off. The house has been empty for a few days.

Kathy (68) *enters, followed by* **Jules (70)**. **Jules** *carries* **Kathy**'s *travel bag.*

Kathy No, the meter thing, the lekky – I should put some money on the key.

Jules Want me to take it down the shop for yer? Drive down Tesco, only take me five minutes –

Kathy No no, it's fine, I'll need to pick up milk later anyway. If I can make it to Venice n' back on my own then I'm sure I can manage Barnsley Road. Bloody Indiana Jones 'ere.

Jules Okay then, / if yer sure.

Kathy / Thanks for pickin' me up. Sorry no, I know I keep sayin' that.

Jules Oh no –

Kathy No, I mean it. Didn't know who else to call, what with Rebecca away. It was all 'er idea.

Jules Can't have yer hitch-hikin' all the way from Manchester Airport now can we?

Kathy Next time I'll stick to Cleethorpes. 'Ey, we should do that together shunt we? We should go on 'oliday together next time, eh, Bri? Be like the old days. Yer know you're the first person I've spoken to all week.

Jules I only ever chat to meself these days. (*Peers into the living room, then –*) Anythin' for a friend –

Kathy Sure yer won't stay for a cuppa a cuppa?

Jules Oh no –

Kathy Get the lekky back on, catch up?

Jules No, I should probably / be gettin' off if I'm honest.

Kathy Expect yer knackered all that drivin' I expect you are. Plus, it's way past my bedtime n'I've a busy start tomorrow, you know me.

Jules I'll see yer around, Kath.

Jules *kisses* **Kathy** *on the cheek.*

Jules Hashtag metoo.

Kathy Hashtag metoo – yeah, um . . .

Jules *exits.*

Kathy Hashtag who, sorry?

The front door is heard, closing shut.

Kathy *stands alone in the dark.*

She tries the lightswitch again.

No use.

Kathy *pulls her mobile phone from her pocket.*

She turns the torch on.

Shines the torch into the living room.

She sees the living room has been trashed.

Things stolen. Furniture turned over. Bottles and drug paraphernalia scattered about the place.

Kathy Oh no. Oh, Mike.

Shines the torch around the room.

Kathy Oh, Mike, **yer'll fuckin' . . . –**

Kathy (69) **– 'ave to wait till** I get back, I don't have time / for this, I don't have time.

Maya (18) But I need you to listen to me, gran, it's important. Can't I just stay with you for a few days?

Kathy *frantically looks for her coat.*

2019

Friday December 13th (Day)

Kathy (69) *getting ready for work, is interrupted by* **Maya (18)** *has recently arrived. She now has green or yellow hair. Dressed like Billie Eilish, carrying a large rucksack.*

Maya Gran, please –

Kathy (69) Look, I'm about to miss my bus, and I'm not – not gettin' involved anymore. For god's sake yer've only been there one term.

Maya (18) Yeah and have you ever –

Kathy *exits into the hall.*

Maya – been to Bristol? It's got the biggest suicide rate of every uni in the country.

Kathy (*off*) Well, everyone finds university hard at first. Leavin' home for the / first time, Mike –

Maya Hard yeah, stressful. When you're having to work all evenings and weekends to pay for some piece o'shit dorm with paper-thin walls. And when –

As **Maya** *speaks,* **Kathy** *re-enters – with her coat – now, looking for her keys.*

Maya – none of it matters anyway because Corbyn's just lost the election, the planet's fuckin' dyin' and they still don't give jobs – the good jobs – to people who didn't go to Oxford. Preferably a white male or some token black Tory on a Stormzy scholarship while the rest of us wait for another Grenfell.

Kathy Look, yer eighteen years old, Maya love, yer've just got to be careful, yer've just –

Maya *hands* **Kathy** *her keys* (*off the coffee table*).

Kathy – got to be careful, haven't you, eh? Yer've just / got to be careful.

Maya Careful, yeah – I've been shut up in those dorms for weeks. I don't like the course, I've made one friend since I got there and she's constantly on ket.

Kathy Then yer need to speak to yer mum. Speak to Melinda, um –

Maya Melissa, and they're out in New Zealand on mum's Indigenous drama project for three month. I have literally no idea who I am or if I'm ever goin' to feel normal again.

Kathy Well, I don't know, I don't know / anythin' about that, –

Maya Please, Gran, 'the right thing'?

Maya / No, I don't know either, I need to sleep. My recovery skill's fucked and my counsellor – there's this supposed counsellor at uni and all she does is email me podcasts or suggest meds to improve my social anxiety and when I just don't like people very much – like, all I want to do is stick my headphones in and watch *Selling Sunset* or *Drag Race*. Is that bad?

Kathy Bad no, I've got patients, **seriously ill patients and I'm –**

Kathy (69) (*on the landline*) **– late, Jessie, I'm late.** About ten or fifteen minutes late . . . Yeah no, I've –

Kathy *takes the remote control and – as she speaks – turns the music down.*

Kathy (*cont., on the landline*) – got yer pills, I've got yer pills . . . The pills, Jessie, –

2020

Monday February 10th (Day)

The TV is on – music channel playing "Own It" by Stormzy.

There's a plastic bag (of groceries, tinned goods) on the coffee table.

Kathy (69) – *in her carer's uniform (polo shirt with Elder Care logo) – is on the landline to an elderly client.*

As she speaks, **Kathy** *pulls an ID pin from her pocket and attaches it to her top.*

Kathy (*cont., on the landline*) – the ones you liked. The pills and yer clean sheets and the bits from Lidl. Now can yer make sure make sure make sure. (*Taps her own head.*) Can yer take the keys out for me, please? . . .

Her mobile phone – from the hallway – starts to ring.

Kathy (*cont., on the landline*) The keys in yer front door, Jessie, yes . . . No, the keys on the inside, on your side . . . Well it means I can come straight in, it –

As **Kathy** *speaks, she picks up the remote control and turns the TV off. The mobile still rings.*

Kathy (*cont., on the landline*) – means I come straight in. . . . No, I know, I know that, yes, I'll –

Kathy *exits into the hall.*

Kathy (*cont., off, on the landline*) – be on the bus. The number 97 bus, the number 97 –

Kathy *re-enters, speaking on the landline, holding the ringing mobile phone.*

Kathy (*cont., on the landline*) – it stops at the bottom of Southey Green Road – yer'll just have to trust me, Brian, I'm much much much much much –

Kathy *answers the mobile phone.*

Kathy (*on the mobile*) Hello, sorry – . . . Hi, yeah, give me two shakes, my lovely.

She puts her ear to the landline.

Kathy (*on the landline*) Sorry, Jessie, I'll be two shakes two shakes two shakes . . . Stay there okay? –

She puts her ear to the mobile.

Kathy (*on the mobile*) Who, sorry, Michael Milne? . . . Hello? . . . No no no, that's right, . . . That's right his mother yes.

Which programme, where? . . . Well, I don't know any Greens, it's a what centre, sorry? No, I haven't seen him, I haven't seen him, I don't know about any programme – in years, love, – six seven years – . . .

The doorbell rings.

Kathy (*on the mobile*) Sorry, no wait for me there –

Kathy *puts the mobile down, takes the landline.*

Kathy (*cont., on the landline*) – Yer still there, love? . . . No no, yer speakin' to Kathy, my love –

As she speaks, **Kathy** *takes the remote control – turns the TV on.*

Kathy (*cont., on the landline*) – Kathy from the care centre, yer daughter's no longer with us, is she?

. . . Yes, well, I'm –

As she speaks, she takes the remote and turns the TV volume down.

Kathy (*cont., on the phone*) – sure she's with God I'm sure she's with God I'm sure . . .

Kathy *thwacks herself on the head, as . . .*

Kathy (*cont., off*) – you're my favourite my favourite, let me get out get out get . . . Out, let me get out, let me get out . . . **The thing, the keys, the –**

2020

<u>Monday March 23rd (Evening)</u>

The room is empty, but the TV is on – BBC News, Prime Minister Boris Johnson's announcement . . .

TV (**Boris Johnson**) That is why people will only be allowed to leave their home for the following very limited purposes: shopping for basic necessities as infrequently as possible. One form of exercise a day – for example –

Kathy *pulls her mobile phone from her dressing gown pocket and dials a number.*

TV (**Boris Johnson**) (*cont.*) a run, walk, or cycle – alone or with members of your household; any medical need, to provide care or to help a vulnerable person; and travelling to and from work, but only where this is absolutely necessary and –

She waits for her call to be answered.

The call is answered . . .

Kathy (70) (*on phone*) Elder Care, it's Elder Care. . . . Yes, my –

She turns the TV volume down, refers to a piece of paper that she's scribbled on as she speaks.

Kathy (*on phone*) **– . . . keep her breathin'**, keep her breathin'. . . . Ventilator, right, good-o. Good-o, good, keep her right, keep her breathin' . . . **– No no, not –**

2020

Wednesday April 8th (Morning)

Kathy *on her landline.*

2020

Monday April 27th (Night)

Kathy *on her mobile.*

Kathy (*on her mobile*) – , **immediate family immediate** family, no, I understand . . . Understand that, love, yes – immediate – no, not immediate. A message, the thing the thing the thing the thing . . .

The thing, the book, the burial – a message for the burial, just stop stop stop . . . Stop fuckin' **interruptin' me, I'm –**

Neighbours (*off*) – **thank you!** / Thank you! / Up the NHS! / Here's to our nurses! / Thank you! / NHS NHS!

Kathy *puts the phone down.*

2020

<u>Thursday April 30th (Early Evening)</u>

The sound of **Neighbours** *applauding/cheering and banging saucepans from outside.*

The noise of the **Neighbours** *dies down.*

Long pause, until . . .

Silence.

Kathy *makes to sleep, when –*

There's a polite 'knock-knock-knock' on the front door, offstage.

Safiya (*off*) 'Ere, Kath? Kathy, are you in?

Pause.

Safiya (*as she enters*) It's Safiya from next door. Yer know yer front door's open, don't yer?

She tap-tap-taps on the front door.

Safiya (*off*) I brought one or two things round for yer. Packet o'party rings, tea bags, milk. Oh, and a few leftovers from dinner last night. Lamb suqaar, a couple o'flatbreads.

Sorry, I haven't seen you out the back for a few days. Is everythin' alright?

Pause.

Safiya (*off*) Lookin' wild out there now with all the sunshine. Thought about choppin' it back for yer, the bushes. Cup o'tea together, watch the birds.

Pause.

Safiya (*off*) Well, yer know where I am, don't yer? You take care, okay? I'll leave the bags in the hall.

Long pause.

Kathy Home again home again, jiggety jig.

Pause.

Kathy Home again **home again, jiggety –**

Kathy **– wobbly, Brian has a** wobbly. . . . "Course 'e's old enough, stop babyin' 'im for once" . . . Off yer pop off yer pop off yer pop to bed now, Michael love, there's Ricicles in top cupboard. . . . Cut 'is toast into soldiers – wheeee. Sleep now, fast asleep. Here's a house, there's the door. Humpty, Hamble n' –

2020

Thursday April 30th (Late Night)

Kathy (70) *still on the sofa.*

An ambulance drives past the house, illuminating the space with its lights.

Kathy (70) And then what. And then what. 1976, 1977 . . .

Kathy *counts her fingers.*

Kathy '74, September '74, '75 . . . '75 . . . '78, Brian, the bins, take out the bins, take yer to the Interchange, Becca. The time, love, **the time – it's –**

Rebecca (*on FaceTime*) **Half seven in the morning, Mum,** there's a twelve-hour time difference.

Kathy No no, I can see yer, love. Smart room it looks, very smart.

Rebecca (*on FaceTime*) Thanks, yeah, it's, um . . . (*She yawns.*) surrounded by mountains. Glenorchy, down in the South. They filmed *Lord of the Rings* round 'ere. Glenorchy, yer can Google it.

2020

Tuesday May 12th (Evening)

Kathy (70), *in her dressing gown, on the sofa.*

Mobile phone in hand, on a FaceTime call with **Rebecca (46)**.

Kathy Okay yes . . . –

Rebecca (*on FaceTime*) Looks more impressive on Google anyway. Three months turns into six. More like *The Shinin'* than the *Lord of the Rings*.

Pause.

Rebecca (*on FaceTime*) Mum?

Kathy Okay, yep, I can see yer, I can see yer –

Rebecca (*on FaceTime*) Livin' off pastries, three-mile hike every day, it's . . . All gettin' a bit weird now. Melissa's taken up vapin'.

Kathy Okay, well as long as yer careful, long as yer careful.

Rebecca (*on FaceTime*) Yer keep freezin', sorry. The screen, yer keep freezin' in time, the signal keeps goin'. – Oh wait, I can see yer now.

Kathy Can yer see me now?

Rebecca (*on FaceTime*) Yeah, I can see yer fine now, thanks. Saw everyone clappin' for the NHS the other night. On the news, I mean, – Fuck, yer not ill are yer? Is that why yer callin'?

Kathy Oh no –

Rebecca (*on FaceTime*) No?

Kathy No no no, the weather the weather –

Rebecca (*on FaceTime*) Well I don't know, they're easin' restrictions so we'll be on the first flight we can get. Maya says she'll be able to get up from Bristol in a week or two.

Kathy / Well, you just let me know, love, let me –

Rebecca (*on FaceTime*) Yeah sure, no . . . (*She yawns a big yawn.*)

Kathy Far too big for me, far too many rooms.

Rebecca (*on FaceTime*) Hm?

Short pause.

I can 'ear yer but yer lips aren't movin'.

Kathy Far too big for me, love, far too many rooms.

Long pause.

Becca –

Rebecca (*on FaceTime*) Yeah, yer back now, Mum, yer went again. – 'Ey, yer know Melissa's mum's started an online fitness class and she's six years older than you. I could send you the link if yer want? Said she's plannin' on doin' the Pennine Way once things are back to normal. Forty-five minutes every mornin', yer can do it from yer phone.

Pause.

Mum –

Kathy I don't know, I –

Rebecca (*on FaceTime*) Mum, wait, / hold on a second.

Kathy I don't know anythin' about that at all at all at all.

Pause.

Sorry, love, it's all a tangle, I'm . . . all all all a bit of a tangle.

Pause.

Goin' back over stuff, all the stuff . . . The stuff I . . . Goin' over stuff, it's all fragments.

Pause.

My choice. My choice, Becs. Them years.

Pause.

Tell 'im I'm sorry. Mike, Michael – tell 'im won't yer, Becs?

Pause.

Becca –

Pause.

Becca, help.

Rebecca (*on FaceTime*) / Ah cool, yer went again. Sorry, I were clickin' refresh, but it wouldn't refresh. Can yer still hear me?

Kathy Yes? / Hello?

Rebecca (*on FaceTime*) / Yer keep freezin', Mum, the screen. What were yer sayin' about the house? – Look, I'll speak to Maya n'make sure she pops over when she's back, alright?

Pause. – **Kathy** *puts the phone aside.*

Rebecca (*on FaceTime*) Mum?

Kathy *buries her head in her hands.*

Rebecca (*on FaceTime*) Are yer still there?

Scrunches her unkempt hair, dragging her fingers through it, as –

<u>**MUSIC – "THIS WOMAN'S WORK" BY KATE BUSH**</u>

Long pause, as the music begins to play over the scene.

Rebecca (*on FaceTime*) Alright, well, I should probably go back now.

Pause.

– Mum?

Kathy *sits up, and tries to shut down the laptop, until . . .*

Rebecca (*on FaceTime*) Alright, so I'll hopefully see you soon, Mum, okay?

Kathy *shuts down the computer, and as "This Woman's Work" goes into its first chorus,* **Kathy** *he pulls herself to her feet.*

She tries to tidy/straighten up the living room with difficulty.

At the end of the first chorus of "This Woman's Work", **Kathy** *continues tidying/clearing the living room, and –*

We hear/see **Rajesh (67)** *and* **Jules (71)** *on Zoom calls, through the song's "Give Me" section.*

Rajesh (67) (*on Zoom*) – **goin' spare** if I'm honest with yer, Kath, I'm on Season Eight of *The Walking Dead* n'I only started watchin' it Monday. Keep havin' showers just to make the day more interestin'. **'Course,** Boris reckons they're gettin' closer to a vaccine, not that I believe a word 'e says. Him n'Matt Hancock – all one big party to them. Never known a bigger **bunch of clowns in me life, not . . . –**

Rebecca (46) – **until we can get** back home. We'll be home soon, Mum, I promise. Just try **n' keep –**

Jules (71) (*on Zoom*) – **since 'e died.** Goin' back, goin' over everythin'. And sometimes yer drift off n' the stupidest things are so vivid. Oh god, you know what I'm talkin' about, I know you know. **While yer –**

Maya (18) (*on Zoom*) – **hey-a, Gran,** are yer still there? It's still thirty-two degrees here **in Bristol, and –**

Jules (*on Zoom*) – **I was so angry** with you, Kath. How come someone who does so much for everyone still manages to do **so little for herself. When / we all –**

Rajesh (*on Zoom*) – **drinkin' champagne** behind closed doors while the rest of us bake banana bread in our jimmy-jams. Could bring some over if yer like? Mark it as my day's essential exercise.

Maya (*on Zoom*) – / **we all** miss you.

(*Pauses.*)

I've missed yer.

(*Pauses*)

Missed us, I mean. Like it was, yer know?

And the song's second chorus is erupting into the lyric "I should be crying, but I just can't let it show", as –

Kathy *sits on the sofa, and – all around her (accompanied by the song's final chorus) –*

The living room is transformed into . . .

. . . the small back garden of the house.

Kathy*'s sofa becomes a garden chair, and . . .*

There's a back wall to the house, with a doorway leading to the kitchen.

A fence that separates **Kathy** *and* **Safiya***'s garden.*

Safiya*'s garden has a washing line, pegged with washing.*

A patio area with garden furniture, and –

Tools and junk and old bags of compost on the patio area. It's not neat or pretty.

A tray of small pots on the garden table, and bags of tomato plant seeds.

At the edge of the patio area, the edge of the lawn/garden which is basic and unkempt.

Kathy *reaches across the table and pulls one of the small pots close to her, as . . .*

"This Woman's Work" By Kate Bush fades out, and the scene becomes . . .

2023

Friday July 21st

A very sunny afternoon.

Mainly the sound of birds, and nearby (occasional) road traffic.

On the garden table, the portable radio plays a news report quietly –

Kathy (73), *sitting by the garden table, has a tray of small pots and a bag of seeds.*

She opens the seeds and pours them onto the table.

She pokes/prods a little hole in one of the small pots.

Then she takes some of the seeds and buries them in the pot.

She covers the seeds up with the soil, then . . .

With a little watering can, pours some water on the seeds.

She moves onto the second pot, as . . ..

Rajesh (70) (*off*) – . . . almost there, come on.

Sound of footsteps, heavy lifting from the kitchen.

– Yer got it?

Mike (53) (*off*) Got it, yeah.

Rajesh *and* **Mike** *enter, through the kitchen doorway, carrying a bathtub full of junk – including boxes. It's quite heavy.* **Rajesh** *comes out first, walking backwards.*

Mike (*off*) Mind yer don't trip on the step. You alright?

Rajesh (*as he enters*) Yeah, . . . yeah, I'm good, um . . .

Both **Mike** *and* **Rajesh** *emerge, carrying the bathtub.*

Looking over his shoulder, **Rajesh** *looks for somewhere to place the bathtub.*

Rajesh . . . try not t'flatten any of 'er plants.

Mike Down there.

Rajesh *tries to see where he means.*

Mike By the fence, down there.

Rajesh Okay, 'ang on, just . . .

Rajesh *steps carefully onto the lawn area, avoiding any plants, and . . .*

He and **Mike** *lower the bathtub onto the patio area, next to the waist-high fence that separates* **Kathy**'*s garden from* **Safiya**'*s neighbouring garden.*

Rajesh (*lowering it*) There we go . . . –

The bathtub lands on the patio with a scrape.

Mike Perfect.

Rajesh Perfect, yep, . . . (*Catches his breath.*) . . . do for now anyway.

Mike Yep.

Mike *pulls a bottle of water from his jeans pocket and takes a small swig.*

He offers it to **Rajesh**.

Rajesh Thanks, no –

Mike I'll start on the rest.

Rajesh Yeah, good, I'll –

Mike *exits, back into the kitchen.*

Rajesh – be with yer, Mike, one tick.

Rajesh *catches his breath, wipes his brow. There's a cut on his finger that stings.*

Pause.

Kathy *is still planting the seeds in her pots, as . . .*

Rajesh *bends over, rummages in the bathtub, looking for a pack of plasters – amongst the bits of pipe, rolls of tube, various tools, bits of paperwork, but . . .*

There is **Brian***'s old guitar on top of everything, so* **Rajesh** *picks it up and leans it up against the wall by the kitchen door.*

He moves to the bathtub and rummages through it, as . . .

Mike *re-enters, from the kitchen, carrying a couple of heavy cardboard boxes – full of paper, photos, cassettes, various junk.*

One of the boxes has 'BECS' written on it with marker pen.

He dumps them down on the patio, then . . .

He exits, back into the kitchen, as . . .

Rajesh, *unable to find the plasters, takes out a small roll of blue masking tape instead.*

He unrolls/bites off a piece, then . . .

Sits on the garden chair, opposite **Kathy**, *and wraps the cut on his finger with the tape.*

Pause, as he does this, then . . .

Rajesh (*to* **Kathy**, *of the radio*) You listenin' to this?

Kathy *is still immersed in planting her seeds.*

Rajesh Kathy.

Rajesh *reaches and touches* **Kathy***'s shoulder.*

Rajesh 'Ere, Kath, . . . 'Ey.

Kathy *continues planting her seeds.*

Rajesh Yer listenin' to this rubbish? Tell yer . . . –

As he speaks, **Rajesh** *picks up the portable radio.*

– . . . if I 'ave to listen to one more posh Tory pipin' up about the economy or Putin or . . . –

He turns the dial on the radio, to find another station.

. . . stoppin' the boats n' sendin' some poor migrant to Rwanda when all they 'ave to do is tax a . . . –

He finds a Classic FM station, playing something mellow (and obvious) like "Clair de Lune".

– . . . couple of fuckwit billionaires and we'd all be better off.

Pleased with his choice of station . . .

There, –

He places the radio back where it was.

– and the world's a better place already.

He strokes **Kathy***'s shoulder again, then . . .*

Finishes strapping the cut on his finger with the masking tape, with the music playing.

With **Kathy** *continuing to plant the seeds,* **Rajesh** *now wrestles his mobile phone out of his pocket.*

He taps and scrolls, checking cinema times or e-tickets.

Pause, as he does this then . . .

Rajesh (*to* **Kathy**) Two o'clock.

Pause – taps and scrolls.

Rajesh Have to be on the bus by two, that gives us . . .

As he speaks, **Mike** *re-enters, with another two boxes and a disused/broken shoe rack that has fallen apart, which he plonks on the patio with the other stuff.*

One of the boxes has 'BRIAN' written in marker pen on it.

Rajesh (*cont.*) . . . about twenty minutes before we go in and get ready, okay?

Pause.

Okay, Kathy?

Kathy *sprinkles seeds on* **Rajesh***'s head.*

Rajesh Funny, yeah, Twenty minutes –

Mike S'alright, that's everythin' from the hallway anyway. Just a couple more –

As they speak, **Safiya** *enters (barely noticed by the guys) from her kitchen and enters her adjoining small garden. She carries an empty washing basket and peg bag.*

Through the next – until indicated – **Safiya** *takes down the washing that is hanging from her line and folds/piles it up in the washing basket.*

Mike (*cont.*) – bits on the landin' n'they should be able to get around easy.

Rajesh Does it matter?

Mike I dunno, ask Rebecca when she gets 'ere. Bin-bag o'recyclin' n' a few books.

Rajesh Not a deal-breaker then.

Mike She can shift it 'erself if she's unhappy.

Mike *pulls a pouch of tobacco from his pocket.*

He leans against the kitchen/back door and, over the next, rolls himself a cigarette.

Rajesh *cleans some of the seeds and soil* **Kathy** *has spilled onto the garden table, scooping them up into his hands.*

Long pause, until . . .

Rajesh *gets up and brushes his hands clean onto the lawn.*

As he does so . . .

Rajesh (*to* **Mike**, *of the bath*) Fuckin' heavy that thing.

Mike What?

Rajesh Fuckin' heavy that thing.

Mike Yeah.

Rajesh *moves and exits into the kitchen, and . . .*

Mike *pops the cigarette in his mouth, switches the radio off (leaving the sound of running taps from the kitchen and the noise of birds singing in the garden), then . . .*

He searches his pockets for a lighter, making brief eye contact with **Safiya** *over the fence –*

Safiya Alright?

Mike Alright, yeah . . . lighter.

Safiya What?

Mike *mimes lighting a lighter.*

Safiya Oh right, can't 'elp yer there, sorry.

Mike *bends down to the boxes.*

He shifts one of them – the one that says 'BRIAN' on the side with marker pen – moving it out of the way, close to **Kathy***'s feet, and . . .*

Rummages around in the box of junk under it, looking for a lighter or matches, as . . .

Kathy *reaches down to the 'BRIAN' cardboard box.*

She opens the lid and makes to take something out, when . . .

Rajesh *re-enters from the kitchen, holding a plate of biscuits and a glass of juice . . .*

He places on the garden table, before **Kathy**, *then exits, as . . .*

Mike (*to* **Rajesh** *as he exits*) Seen my yellow cricket anywhere, Raj?

No answer from **Rajesh**, *and . . .*

As **Kathy** *takes and eats one of the biscuits,* **Mike** *gives up on the lighter, and . . .*

Throws his rolled cigarette onto the lawn.

He takes a swig from his bottle of water, then . . .

Sees and moves to the old guitar, leant against the wall.

He picks it up, looks at it, then . . .

Sits down on the garden chair, opposite, **Kathy**, *and places the guitar on his lap.*

Pause, as . . .

Mike *strums a couple of chords – G and Em, a bit of C and F.*

Safiya *– having finished taking the washing down – is about to exit with the washing basket.*

Safiya Dint know yer played.

Mike Hm? Oh . . . –

Safiya Sounds / nice.

Mike / No, um . . . Thanks, no I don't. They 'ad one down the Greens, the old, um . . . rehab when I were there, picked up a couple o'chords, um . . .

He demonstrates.

Musical therapy the lad called it. G and E minor, I'm . . . hardly Ed Sheeran or owt.

Safiya Nice to be able to play an instrument.

Mike Yeah no, it is a bit.

Safiya *exits into her house, carrying the washing basket as . . .*

Mike *continues strumming the guitar, while . . .*

Kathy *watches him, eating her biscuit.*

Long pause, as . . .

Mike *extends his chord pattern, from G to Em to C and D, and back again, and . . .*

Kathy*, softly, starts humming along. So softly that* **Mike** *doesn't notice.*

This continues for a few moments, then . . .

Rajesh*, in just his boxer shorts and a Salmon shirt, enters, holding* **Mike***'s mobile phone.*

He places the mobile phone on the garden table, before **Mike***, with . . .*

Rajesh Yer sister messaged.

Mike *nods, as* **Rajesh** *exits as quickly as he entered, and . . .*

Continues to strum the chord pattern on the guitar.

Kathy*'s humming gets a bit louder . . .*

Kathy (*sings*) Mm-mm mm-m my lovely,
Mm-mm-mm in your bed,
Tell me thoughts mmmmhh ,
Mmm, mmm, mmm yes I do . . ..

Kathy*'s humming/singing fades out, and she takes another bite of biscuit, but . . .*

Mike *has heard her, and plays with a bit more confidence to encourage her to keep going.*

Long pause, as he does so, then . . .

Knock-knock-knock-knock – from the front door, inside the house – but . . .

He keeps playing the guitar anyway, as . . .

Rajesh (*off*) Think that's them now, Mike!

Pause.

'Ere, Mike!

Knock-knock-knock-knock – from the front door, inside the house -, and . . .

Rajesh (*off*) Alright, hold on, I'm comin'!

Mike *gradually stops playing and climbs to his feet.*

He rests the guitar against the back wall, and switches the radio back on – Classic FM – and takes another gulp from his water bottle.

He exits inside the house, leaving . . .

Kathy *sitting at the garden table, eating her biscuit, which . . .*

After a few moments, she places down on the plate, and . . .

Reaches down for the cardboard box marked 'BRIAN' again.

She rummages inside and takes out one or two items – a work tie, a tobacco tin, a CD of "Hounds of Love", a small bottle of aftershave – placing them carefully on the garden table.

With the music on the radio still playing, she takes the tobacco tin and opens the lid.

Removes a Zippo lighter, and makes to hand it to **Mike**, *but . . .*

Mike *isn't there, so she puts it down.*

She looks in the tin, and pulls out a pre-rolled spliff.

She smells it.

Pause, then . . .

She puts it in her mouth, then takes the Zippo lighter.

She lights the lighter and lights the spliff.

Kathy *takes one or two drags of the spliff, when . . . –*

Estate Agent (*on entering*) Mm, yeah, I suppose they are all very classic –

The **Estate Agent** (*played by the same actor who played* **Brian**) *enters, followed by the* **Young Man** *and* **Young Woman**.

Estate Agent (*cont.*) – layouts on this road, they're all from pretty much the same / period I know that much.

Young Man / Edwardian I guess?

Estate Agent (*to* **Kathy**) Hi there, sorry. (*To the* **Young Man**.) Late Victorian most likely.

Young Woman Nice big garden, Emil, look. / (*To* **Kathy**.) Ooh sorry, god, excuse me.

Young Man Oh, excellent, it's massive. Just /

Young Woman Yep, pretty big, lots like your mum's garden, look. Potential.

Young Woman (*to* **Kathy**) Sorry, do you mind if we look around . . . ?

Mike (*on entering*) No no, don't mind us, love, you go ahead.

Mike *enters, carrying the bin-bag of recycling he mentioned earlier, and . . .*

. . . as the **Young Man** *and* **Young Woman** *step onto the lawn, looking onto the garden . . .*

. . . he dumps the bin-bag down and, on seeing **Kathy**, *rushes over to her, and takes the spliff out of her hand, placing it on the biscuit plate.*

Young Man Room for a work shed.

Young Woman Oh shuddup 'work shed'. Man-cave more like.

Estate Agent Ha, well summer houses are becoming more popular.

Pause, as they look around.

Estate Agent (*gesticulates to go inside*) Do you want to keep lookin', get a feel / for the place?

Young Woman / Ooh, yes please – /

Young Man Likin' it so far, lots of potential.

Estate Agent Go ahead, I'll leave you to it. Any questions, just –

The **Young Man** *and* **Woman** *exit back into the house.*

Estate Agent (*cont.*) – give me a shout, okay?

Pause, and **Estate Agent** *turns to* **Mike**, *and . . .*

Chuckles, rolls his eyes, pulling his mobile phone from his pocket.

Mike Seem keen.

Estate Agent Yep, oh yep.

Awkward pause.

Sorry we were a bit behind by a / few minutes.

Mike / No no, bang on time, mate, bang on time.

The **Estate Agent** *checks his phone – tapping/scrolling, work stuff.*

Mike *and* **Kathy** *are both watching him.*

Pause.

Mike Sell many properties round this way, d'yer?

No response. The **Estate Agent** *is engrossed in his phone, so . . .*

Mike *makes to take the biscuit plate, when . . .*

His phone vibrates – a message.

Mike *grabs the phone and . . .*

Mike (*to* **Kathy**) Swampy's arrived.

. . . he makes to exit, as . . .

Estate Agent Hm, sorry? Do we sell many others did yer say? Sorry, I –

Mike (*as he goes*) That's alright, mate, you carry on.

Mike *exits, and . . .*

The **Estate Agent** *returns to his phone, tapping and scrolling.*

Pause, and . . .

Kathy *takes the spliff from the biscuit plate, puts it in her mouth, as . . .*

Glued to his phone, the **Estate Agent** *sits on the chair, opposite* **Kathy**.

Pause, as . . .

Kathy *lights the spliff again and smokes, watching the* **Estate Agent**, *who . . .*

Keeps tapping/scrolling on his phone.

Pause.

The **Estate Agent** *finally finishes sending his text message and puts the phone in his pocket.*

He sees **Kathy** *staring at him. Smiles.*

Kathy *smiles back and offers the spliff to him.*

Kathy Hurdy Gurdy.

Pause.

Hurdy Gurdy.

Estate Agent Oh . . .

The **Estate Agent** *hesitates.*

He almost goes to take it, then makes a gesture to decline, when . . .

Kathy *grabs hold of his hand, squeezing it.*

Pause, and . . .

Rebecca (49) *enters, with a bag of shopping and a* **Kathy***'s hospital crutch.*

She makes to say something, but stops when she sees **Kathy** *holding the* **Estate Agent***'s hand.*

Kathy Yer can go now, Bri.

Pause.

Go on . . .

Mike *enters, holding the pile of books he mentioned earlier.*

Kathy . . . get off now, get / the number 97 bus –

Rebecca (49) / Hey Mum, how yer doin'? –

Rebecca *gives* **Kathy** *a kiss on the head and pulls her hand free from the* **Estate Agent**.

Rebecca (*cont.*) – Raj says he's taking yer to the cinema tonight, that's exciting isn't it?

And the **Estate Agent** *moves up and out the chair and exits back into the house, as . . .*

Mike *takes the spliff from* **Kathy**'s *hand and stubs it out with his foot, while –*

Rebecca *moves and sits in the chair, opposite* **Kathy**, *with –*

Rebecca (*cont.*) Lucky I've brought yer good crutch along for yer, I reckon. Bet you haven't been down the Odeon in a while.

Rebecca *mouths 'what the fuck?' to* **Mike**, *who shrugs.*

Rebecca Buy a big box of popcorn, can't yer?

Mike She's not a kid, fuckin' 'ell.

Rebecca Wish I was comin' to see *Barbie*, I'm partial to a bit of Margot Robbie meself.

Rebecca *mouths 'go up and see them' to* **Mike**, *who ignores her.*

Rebecca (*to* **Kathy**) 'Ere, look what I got yer, look.

Rebecca *reaches into her shopping bag and pulls out a silly pink wig.*

Rebecca – Party section in Wilko's. Thought yer'd best look the part.

Rebecca *tries the wig on for size.*

Should've got one meself.

Mike Well, it's an improvement I suppose. Middle-aged Dyke Barbie.

Rebecca Mm, that's rich comin' from Divorced Junkie Incel Barbie. (*Makes to put the wig on* **Kathy**.) Shall we try it on for size?

Mike *swipes the wig from* **Rebecca**.

Rebecca 'Ey, just stop it now, Mike, that's –

Mike *tosses the wig into the garden.*

Over the next, **Kathy** *takes her crutch with one hand and picks up her tray of small pots with the other. Unnoticed by her kids, she gets up and starts moving towards to the lawn area.*

Rebecca (*cont.*) – actually brand new.

Mike She's not wearin' it.

Rebecca Oh come on, have a sense of / occasion –

Mike / You are not dressin' 'er up like some Chinese fuck-off poodle.

Rebecca Eh? Which Chinese – ?

Mike Not while I'm around, no.

Rebecca Mike . . . –

Mike No.

Rebecca (*retrieves the wig*) Oh my god –

Mike Fuckin' no, Rebecca, no. –

Rajesh *re-enters, dressed in a pink combination, sticking his head round the door.*

Mike (*cont.*) – I swear to god, if you try that again –

Rajesh 'Ey, sssh! Are you two tryin' to scare them away or somethin'?

They stop.

Pause.

Rajesh *grabs the pink wig and puts it on.*

Bollywood Barbie, ta-dah. 'Ere, Kath . . .

Mike *and* **Rebecca** *see* **Kathy** *is heading to the lawn with her tray of pots.*

Rajesh Reckon yer could still fancy us in this? 'Ere, Kath.

She doesn't respond.

Rajesh *chucks the pink wig at* **Mike**, *who catches it.*

Rajesh (*as he does so*) Behave will yer? Keep yer voices down.

Rajesh *exits.*

Rebecca (*to* **Mike**) Don't say it.

Mike What?

Rebecca Whatever it is yer goin' to say, don't say it.

Rebecca *moves over to* **Kathy**.

Rebecca 'Ey, come on, let me help . . . –

She takes the tray of small pots and helps **Kathy** *crouch onto the lawn.*

Rebecca Stop yer havin' another accident –

Mike *joins his sister, helping* **Kathy** *down onto the lawn.*

Pause, as they do so.

Rebecca (*to* **Kathy**) How's that, better?

Kathy *nods, reaching for her gardening trowel.*

She starts to dig a trench in the soil for the pots to go, and . . .

Rebecca *starts carefully taking the pots out of the tray, as . . .*

Mike *takes* **Kathy***'s crutch, and leans it up against the chair, then . . .*

Sees and pockets the Zippo lighter, and . . .

Picks up the cardboard box that is marked 'BECS' and . . .

Moves and sits in **Kathy***'s garden chair, with the box on his lap.*

Long pause, as **Rebecca** *and* **Kathy** *work together planting the pots,* **Mike** *opens the 'BECS' box and rummages around inside, taking out and inspecting items like a set of 80s bangles, a map of Europe, a few photos, and a Duran Duran vinyl single.*

Then . . .

Mike (*as he rummages through the box*) Thought yer'd've got 'ere earlier.

Rebecca Nope.

Pause.

Mike (*as he rummages through the box*) Still got that Ukranian couple stayin' with yer?

No response.

Becs.

Pause.

Becca –

Rebecca There's a spare room at Maya's flat, I've told yer that already.

Mike Maya can't stand me –

Rebecca Have you asked? Yer'd probably get on like an house on fire with 'er new fella n'I know they're lookin' for a guitarist for their new band, if you can call that racket music.

Mike *shifts uncomfortably.*

Rebecca Yes, we've still got the Ukranians for the time bein'. Symon and Lilya. Sorry about that.

Mike Sorry for what, self-righteous virtue signallin'? –

As they speak, **Safiya** *re-enters from her back door, with the washing basket filled with a new batch of recently washed clothes. Over the next, she starts pegging them up on the line.*

Mike – Some of us can't afford Symon and Lilya, I work at Topps Tiles two days a week.

Rebecca So that justifies you bein' a bigot?

Mike Bigot, yeah, like that cartoon of the Star of David covered in blood you posted the other day. My kids are Jewish, don't forget.

Pause.

Lose yer job if yer not careful.

Rebecca Plenty of St George's on your timeline I don't care for either, Mike.

Mike That's a closed group, there's a difference.

Rebecca What, 'Power to the People'?

Mike It's a closed group, and they're real people, not those woke / fuckin' theatre dickheads.

Rebecca / Bunch of football hooligans threatenin' to burn down hotels.

Mike Nope, just one hotel.

Rebecca Make yer feel good, does it? Spreadin' lies n' misinformation –

Mike That makes two of us, Becs, at least I've still got my looks.

Rebecca (*laughs*) Oh my god, have yer looked in a mirror lately? Jesus Christ . . .

Rebecca *chuckles to herself.*

Rebecca I mean, Jesus . . . –

Kathy Yer still very pretty. Yer've always been a pretty girl.

Pause. **Mike** *and* **Rebecca** *stop what they're doing.*

Kathy Pretty sweet. Sweet.

Pause, then . . .

Rebecca Yeah sure, if there's one thing I'm not . . . –

Kathy Dad called yer his 'thousand puddings'. 'Thousand puddings' 'e'd say.

Pause.

Kathy 'There's my thousand puddings.' 'There's my thousand puddings.'

Kathy *hugs* **Rebecca**.

She doesn't let go.

Long pause, then . . .

Rajesh *enters, holding a bright pink jacket.*

He moves over and strokes **Kathy** *on the back.*

Rajesh Hey.

Pause.

Hey, come on now, we've got an Uber on the way. Don't want to miss the trailers, they're the best bit.

Rajesh *helps* **Kathy** *up to her feet, and . . .*

Mike *grabs the crutch and places it in* **Kathy***'s hand.*

Rajesh There we go, that's it.

Rajesh *places the pink jacket on* **Kathy**.

Rajesh Now we both look the part don't we, eh?

Rajesh *gives* **Kathy** *her crutch and helps her toward the kitchen door.*

Rajesh Change yer nappy n'we're good to go. – (*To* **Mike**.) Might want to check on them upstairs, Mike?

Mike Yeah no, gotchya . . .

Mike *gets up, bypasses them, and moves inside, exiting, as . . .*

Rajesh (*calls to* **Mike**, *as he goes*) Should be back by seven or eight if yer still fancy the chip shop.

As they pass, **Kathy** *picks up the watering can and passes it to* **Safiya** *over the fence.*

Safiya Oh, thanks . . .

Rajesh Off we go then, up sticky sticks.

Safiya (*taking the watering can*) . . . thanks, Kathy, love.

Rajesh *takes* **Kathy** *by the arm and leads her into the house.*

Rajesh (*as they go*) Oop, mind the step there, remember?

They exit.

Long pause, as . . .

Safiya *places the watering can down (on her side of the fence), then . . .*

. . . makes to say something to **Rebecca**, *who – still crying, cheeks smudged with mascara – continues planting the pots into the trench, but . . .*

Safiya *decides against it and, taking her washing basket, exits back into her own house.*

Long pause, then . . .

Mike *re-enters.*

He sees **Rebecca**, *then . . .*

Moves to the box marked 'BECS' and removes her E.T. toy (from 1983).

Pause.

He moves over to **Rebecca**, *squats next to her.*

Then, using the toy . . .

Mike Phone hooome.

Pause.

E.T. Phooone –

Rebecca *grabs* **Mike**'*s hand.*

Long pause.

Mike *kisses* **Rebecca**'*s hand.*

Mike Yeah?

Rebecca Yeah.

Pause.

Yeah, thanks, that's . . .

The **Young Man** *and* **Young Woman** *re-enter . . .*

Young Man (*as they enter, to the* **Young Woman**) – . . . in principle we'd be looking for a five year mortgage, yer see?

Young Woman Hm, probably safer / in the short term.

Young Man Safer, yeah, after / Liz Truss bankrupted the country.

Young Woman (*to* **Mike** *and* **Rebecca**) / Sorry, we just wanted another quick look before we left? Do you mind if I take a couple of pictures?

Mike No no, please –

Young Man (*to* **Mike** *and* **Rebecca**) Been livin' in this area long 'ave yer?

Young Woman (*taking her phone out*) / We've just seen so many today, it helps me keep a mental picture, um, image, um, thing.

Mike Oh, well, yeah –

Rebecca We grew up / here.

Mike / Grew up round 'ere, yeah, lots of, um . . . –

Rebecca Memories, yer know.

Mike Two chip shops – one round the back, another up the hill. Five pubs, now there's just The Pitsmoor n'the Bay Horse.

Rebecca This place –

Mike This place, yeah, it's . . .–

Young Man Ten minutes into town which is never a bad thing. – (*To the* **Young Woman**.) I mean, we could dig up this whole patio if we wanted. I reckon **I'd be a bit of dab 'and at –**

Young Man **– tryin' to find a station,** I know it works.

Young Woman Fannyin' around with that radio all night, some old woman's junk. I thought you were goin' to help with bathtime.

Young Man Whose bathtime? Yours or the baby's?

Young Woman (*pulls him up by the arm*) Oh grow up, yer big neanderthal, get into the part.

2024

<u>Wednesday July 24th (Evening)</u>

There's a full moon.

Kathy*'s tomato plants have grown.*

The **Young Man** *sits on the garden chair, holding the vintage radio.*

He turns the dial, trying to find a station.

The **Young Woman** *stands in the kitchen/back doorway.*

Young Man Which part, sorry?

Young Woman Inside, come on, I'm not . . . –

They exit inside – and the **Young Woman** *closes the back door behind them.*

Young Woman (*as they exit*) – . . . doin' this all on my own.

Young Man (*as they exit*) Who said I'm playin' a part? 'Ey . . .

Young Woman (*as they exit*) Everyone plays / a part.

Young Man (*as they exit*) / – don't give me that look, it's a serious question.

The couple's voices fade out.

Phil Oakey's "Together in Electric Dreams" from the radio.

Safiya *enters from her backdoor.*

She peers over the fence, checking her neighbours have gone inside.

Safiya *picks up the watering can.*

She crosses into her new neighbours' garden.

Safiya *waters* **Kathy***'s tomato plants.*

The moon shines above.

Lights fade.\

www.ingramcontent.com/pod-product-compliance
Lightning Source LLC
LaVergne TN
LVHW052340100826
845147LV00021B/1127

9781350635272